## Praise for *Less Over More*

"Tony pours his years of experience as a coach into helping his readers reset their mindsets and create more abundant and fabulous lives. For entrepreneurs who've been busting their butts chasing 'more,' Tony provides a simple and proven path to help them attain the success and fulfillment they've been looking for."

—Jen Sincero, #1 *New York Times* Bestselling Author, *You Are a Badass*

"Tony Caliendo redefines ambition not as the hunger for more, but the clarity and discipline to want better. *Less Over More* is the quiet manifesto for those who've finally realized that depth, joy, and quality always beat volume."

—Jonas Koffler, *New York Times* Bestselling Author, *Hustle*

"Tony's keynote received outstanding feedback and made a meaningful difference for the leaders he worked with. He equips executives with practical tools to create certainty, inspire confidence, and lead effectively amid constant change. Through his Less Over More framework, Tony helps leaders prioritize what truly drives results, stay clear and focused under pressure, and communicate with conviction. He brings ideas together in a way that empowers people to move forward with intention and purpose. Tony's work exemplifies the power of true partnership and the impact a skilled coach can have on an organization."

—Brian King, President, Enterprise Transformation and CALA Marriott International

"This book is a breath of fresh air for anyone who is tired of running hard and still feeling behind. It challenges the belief that the next achievement, the next purchase, the next big thing will finally bring peace. Instead, it makes a strong case that simplicity is not settling, it's selecting what is important to us.

The guidance he gives to us is clear and it is simple to follow.

If life feels crowded, if success has started to feel heavy, or if you are carrying responsibilities without freedom, I believe this book will reset your perspective and give you a plan to follow."

—Dianna Kokoszka, Board Member, John Maxwell Leadership Foundation, and former CEO, MAPS Coaching

"In a world obsessed with accumulation, Tony Caliendo's *Less Over More* delivers a refreshing perspective on abundance, revealing the liberating truth that having less can lead to greater joy, success, and freedom. He guides us to align our lives with what truly matters, fostering authentic relationships and meaningful work. This timely message inspires us to declutter our lives and break free from the relentless pursuit of 'more,' clearing space for clarity, connection, and fulfillment so we finally feel we have enough, and we are enough."

—Robin Fisher Roffer, Founder and CEO, Big Fish Marketing, and Author, *Make a Name for Yourself* and *The Fearless Fish Out of Water*

"*Less Over More* is the kind of book that gently takes you by the shoulders, looks you in the eyes, and says, 'You don't need another thing. You need your life back.' Tony Caliendo doesn't preach minimalism from a mountaintop—he walks you through the cluttered garage of your beliefs, flips on the light, and helps you decide what actually belongs. Practical without being preachy, soulful without being soft, *Less Over More* is a permission slip to stop chasing, start choosing, and finally experience the kind of abundance that doesn't exhaust you. This isn't about having less; it's about becoming more—more honest, more aligned, more alive."

—Tania Katan, Author, *Creative Trespassing*

"*Less Over More* is a powerful reminder that clarity creates momentum.

In a culture obsessed with excess and doing more, Tony makes a compelling case for prioritizing what truly matters and eliminating the unnecessary things that drain focus and dilute results. This is not theory; it is practical guidance for simplifying your decisions, tightening your priorities, and delivering stronger outcomes with greater intention.

What resonated most with me is the freedom that comes from disciplined focus, building real success while living the life you desire.

Less isn't about shrinking your ambition. It's about refining it and the results speak for themselves."

—Suzanne Sakelaris, former Executive, Omnicon-IPG and WPP Media, and New Mexico Nonprofit Leader

"The right book for the right time, *Less Over More* helps motivated individuals get off the 'hamster wheel' of chasing all things, most of which are not making us happier. Tony walks you through an amazing journey of liberation from all those things that we were taught by our parents, mentors, and leaders, and boils it down to the 'quality' that matters versus the 'quantity' that life has served up. I wish I had these techniques when I was raising my kids who are all now in their twenties. Who thought that chasing less and the alignment of our deep values would have such an amazing outcome and trajectory for our remaining time on this planet? Reclaim your time, energy, and SPIRIT today. Thank you, Tony!"

—Fritz Pollard, Director and Executive Coach, The Coaching Nexus

"Over 30 years of friendship and working together, I've seen Tony consistently lead with intention, clarity, and a deep respect for people. *Less Over More* is an invitation to live and lead from 'enough,' clearing mental and material clutter so you can create more meaningful relationships, better energy, and a life you actually enjoy."

—Michael Allard, Hospitality Industry Leader, and Co-Owner, Think Up Consulting

# LESS OVER MORE

# LESS OVER MORE

## How to Rethink Your Path, Reset Your Future, and Rebuild the Life You Love

TONY CALIENDO

Matt Holt Books
An Imprint of BenBella Books, Inc.
Dallas, TX

Matt Holt is an imprint of BenBella Books, Inc.
BenBella Books, Inc.
8080 N. Central Expressway
Suite 1700
Dallas, TX 75206
benbellabooks.com
Send feedback to feedback@benbellabooks.com



Printed in the United States of America
10 9 8 7 6 5 4 3 2 1

Library of Congress Control Number: 2026009153
ISBN 9781637749265 (hardcover)
ISBN 9781637749272 (electronic)

Copyediting by James Fraleigh
Proofreading by Martha Gallant and Ashley Casteel
Text design and composition by PerfecType, Nashville, TN
Cover design by Jason Arias
Printed by Lake Book Manufacturing

*For my family, and for the mentor who trusted this work before it had a name.*

# CONTENTS

## PART IV: ABUNDANCE THROUGH LESS

# INTRODUCTION

## The Gift of Less

More does NOT always create more. But you know what does? Less.

Wait, what? How is this possible, you ask? Because less opens space in our lives for more. *Less creates more.*

I was in my early forties when I learned this life-changing lesson and witnessed the power of "less" as a tool to create space for more. I had the perfect job, amazing health, a great relationship, and a constant drive for success in all areas of my life. From the outside looking in, things were "perfect," and it appeared I had it all. More money, more fun, more love, more success.

Yet, lurking around the corner were changes, some forced and some chosen, that would alter my life and business forever. These were my introduction to less over more, which created more opportunities in my life, and far more growth in my business and my relationships, than I had ever known.

It took me a moment to wrap my head around this paradox, as nothing about it made any sense. This new truth went against all my years of education, coaching, and business training, along with the body of beliefs I had learned and practiced.

I found myself asking, "What if the world has it backward?" What if abundance lies not in the pursuit of more, *but instead in choosing less*—in clearing the unnecessary from your life to make room for the experiences and joys that truly matter?

## THE HIGH COST OF LIVING IN MORE

We live in a world where the cost of everything seems to be skyrocketing—housing, food, healthcare, education. Inflation has made basic necessities feel like luxuries. Yet oddly, we've learned to embrace the lie of more. We chase more things that don't sustain us: more stress, more mindless consumption, more of what ultimately leaves us feeling empty and overwhelmed. We've been conditioned to believe that accumulating more will solve our problems, when in reality, it often creates new ones.

## REDEFINING LESS

This insight forced me to redefine my understanding of less, as well as recast the story I had accepted for what less meant. In my search for new meaning, I came to realize that choosing less, strangely, is *not* about a scarcity mindset. It's not about a loss per se. It is about letting go.

My husband, Reagan, and I were part of a dinner club with a small group of our friends. One fall evening, it was our turn to host. I had announced we'd be making beef bourguignon, having *no* clue how complicated this meal was to prepare. For the recipe, I turned to one of my favorite chefs, Ina Garten. I quickly found myself horrified and overwhelmed by the list of over 17 ingredients and the three pages of cooking instructions. This was *truly* an example of "more": more ingredients, more directions, more steps, more time, more detail. Despite the lengthy list of ingredients and instructions, I trusted the source and followed it to the letter, and it was a triumph.

Once dinner was over, I was sitting at the table surrounded by friends and noticed my finished plate. For the first time, I had a moment to enjoy the stillness of the day, the kind that comes over you when you accomplish a major task.

Then a thought came to me: *Does this empty plate that was full represent my life?* I noticed that lately I had been piling my "plate" high: my business, helping others, saying "yes" to nearly every new opportunity. My schedule was full but my energy was depleted.

I realized that much like my dinner plate, my life and business plate could only hold so much before it overflowed. Yet, the deeper question I had for myself was, "Did I fill the plate and cover all the empty space because of my conditioning of 'more'?" Was I doing these same things in my business, and blocking space to receive what mattered?

That moment changed how I thought about "more." I saw that fullness is not the goal—fulfillment is. You can only consume so much, and what you choose to put on your plate, whether it is food or commitments, should be intentional, meaningful, and aligned with who you truly are.

That night, the empty plate didn't represent lack. It represented possibility—the space to choose what really matters.

Later that night, after my friends had left, and as Reagan and I were washing the mountain of pots and pans, I also began thinking about the opportunities in my life. And I thought, what if life were like the sponge I held in my hands? If you place a sponge under running water, it will absorb it until it is saturated. At this point, the water starts bouncing off the sponge and running down the drain. Until you wring out the sponge and release the excess water, you will prevent the sponge from absorbing more. What if the water is your opportunity, and you are the sponge? There's only so much opportunity you can take on before you must be intentional and wring out the sponge to take on more.

You must intentionally create the space for more (but only the right kind of more) by choosing less. It's not always easy to do, especially when you begin the process, but in the challenge of choosing less, you will find grace and unmatchable calm. Less brings peace. But finding that peace takes work, and first we have to look back at our conditioning.

## BREAKING GENERATIONAL PROGRAMMING

In my case, the move to less was truly challenging. I was raised by first-generation Americans, whose parents were Italian immigrants who arrived in the 1920s and had an extreme belief around scarcity. They would routinely tell me, "Tony, you may never get more . . . so, hold on to what you have." They never considered wringing out the sponge.

Both of my parents were children of the Great Depression and witnessed times of not having enough and of things being taken away from them, from food and furniture to loved ones killed in destructive wars. Those beliefs stayed with them and became part of their programming. That programming then became a part of my operating system while I was young and impressionable, as it did for my siblings.

Each of us held on tightly to what we had, as we did not believe we were capable of more. This meant clinging to possessions like broken items, old plastic butter containers, rubber bands from the evening paper delivery, twisty ties from the bread packaging, jam jars that became drinking glasses, and more. My siblings and I filled our space with "things." We collected what we thought we needed and never let go.

I was visiting my mom in 2017, shortly after my dad had passed, so it was just the two of us. We were hanging out, drinking coffee as usual. She turned to me and said, "Do you mind going down to the basement freezer and grabbing a loaf of bread?" Without hesitation, I headed toward the basement door. I opened it and began moving into what I referred to as my parent's time capsule. I paused for a moment and started taking it all in. A few toys from our childhood, boxes full of memories, and treasures my parents collected over the decades.

As I looked up, something caught my eye—the Mr. Coffee Graveyard! Old machine after old machine placed neatly next to each other like a museum display.

After a few minutes, I snapped out of my Mr. Coffee haze and remembered why I was in the basement: to get the bread! I'm quite certain that my mom was thinking, *What is taking him so long? I'm 87 and could have got my own bread much quicker.*

I walked up the steps, bread in hand and curiosity growing about the old, retired coffee machines. I asked Mom what the story was with all the machines, and she simply said, "You never know when you will need an extra carafe or part of a machine." Of course, in my mind I was processing her trying to "fix" one versus buying a new one. I asked her, wouldn't it just be easier to run down to the store and get a new one? She looked at me as if I had three heads. She didn't see this as an option. You kept what you had and filled up the space with it.

The kicker to this story is, during this same visit, her current machine broke. I was sent to the basement, ego in check, to retrieve one of the "old" machines. There was one in particular she told me to get that still made coffee but the "on/off" button didn't really work, and you just had to plug and unplug it to avoid it burning out. This sent slight terror of a raging fire through my mind.

I believe she enjoyed this moment way too much, seeing me headed to the "time capsule" to learn the value of storing things. This was when I realized that my thinking had evolved from my parents'. It was just one example of the "collecting" mentality and it made me wonder: How many missed opportunities happened in my parents' lifetime simply because they did not have the space for it to show up? Simply because they did not wring out the sponge?

As I went on in my young adult life, I found myself, like many, consuming and gathering. I was going to buck my upbringing and buy *as much as I wanted when I wanted* and join the "consumption" generation. What I didn't realize at the time was all the "stuff" I was gathering was clogging the opening to receive more. I now know that receiving an opportunity happens when you are open and ready to receive it by having the space for it to show up. Like a superhighway during rush hour traffic, if you can't clear a lane, you'll severely delay the arrival of opportunities—or they may never get through at all.

## MY AWAKENING

Less is more for reasons besides the practical. There's a spiritual component and a practice involved as well. I have a strong faith in God, and realized that my choice to fill my plate with stuff was blocking the true blessings that were waiting for me. Blocking my receiving the right opportunity. Blocking my ability to say no to people. Blocking my restraint about buying material goods. God, a higher power, the universe, or whatever you believe was waiting for me to "wring out the sponge" so that I could create the space for more in my life—the right more.

What I didn't fully understand was that I'm not creating this life on my own—I'm cocreating it with God. Asking is only half of the equation; you also have to be ready to receive. And deeper still, I had to ask myself: Was I chasing *my* plan, or walking in *His*? Looking back, I wonder how many opportunities I missed before I learned that lesson.

It wasn't until 2009 when I got the message loud and clear. I had left the real estate team that I led and taken a new role as an investor and leader of a large real estate brokerage. I was faced with the truth that all the "stuff" I was busy doing was not preventing me from failing. This was the first time that I could not fill my plate, and through some luck and a *ton* of work, find my way to some semblance of success.

After struggling for months and coming to terms that I either needed to resign or potentially be let go, I was tossed a life preserver. I shared my woes with a peer, and she encouraged me to enroll in a coaching program. This program was like no other. It addressed programming, habits, and limiting beliefs. It helped identify the "clutter" in my mind, my business, and life, and was my first experience that less can be the multiplier of more.

This program helped me realize that I was defaulting to old habits and had truly detached from current reality. Once I "decluttered" my brain, my activities, and my thoughts, I was on the path to true success. The results and experience were far greater than just receiving more. By moving through a process of clearing, of choosing less and the right kind of more, I was experiencing incredible opportunities, relationships, and growth, yet also a level of peace that I had never felt—ever.

By clearing the clutter, I opened myself up to the things that truly nourished me. I no longer felt depleted at the end of the day. I was a better spouse, friend, son, uncle, brother, and human. It was as if someone flipped a switch and my life truly started to unfold in the way I believed it was meant to, instead of my forced version.

I believe we all have God-given talents and a purpose, yet we cloud our vision and start to buy into our own sense of "just do more" for our perceived good. That cloud happens as our mind is flooded with thoughts, most of which are distracting at best, or harmful at worst.

## THE POWER OF THINKING LESS

"Wait, are you saying what I think you are saying? That it is possible to choose between empowering or disempowering thoughts? That I can choose?" Yes! I spent most of my life holding on to limiting beliefs and old programming of "just do more." Work harder, work longer, skip the vacation, just *do more than anyone else and you will be fine.*

The truth is that changing your thoughts plays a *huge* role in your new existence. When I realized that my thoughts would drive all results and help me eliminate old beliefs and clutter, my path became clear.

I can remember numerous times when I talked to my parents about success and wealth. They would say, "We just aren't those people." I didn't understand. Why aren't we "those" people? Did we get in the wrong line? Did we miss the memo that allowed us to have abundance? My beliefs molded to their beliefs, and I took it as gospel that we weren't "those people."

As I started my journey of "less" and clearing my disempowering thoughts, I could see a different path in front of me. One that I always dreamed of yet couldn't crack the code on how to achieve. I'd feel small glimpses of a different life, yet it was fleeting and would disappear. When it would "leave," I could hear myself say, "Well, Mom and Dad were right, we just aren't those people and that was just a lucky moment." Yet, in my gut, the conviction that I could achieve more struggled with the "how" of doing so.

Rewiring your thoughts takes effort and commitment. To let go of all you have ever known and "programmed" into your beliefs is no small task. In a world that's all about more consumption, it may take more than a moment for you to trust this process. Begin by trusting that *less is the great multiplier of more* and your thoughts around this will affect your success. Once you accept it and see the possibility, you will feel lightness and peace.

If you are ready to experience the joy of doing less and getting more, of having a plate with the right amount of space and a sponge that's ready to absorb, I am excited to share the process with you. The journey you are embarking on with me can be the key to unlocking the mindset, lifestyle, and business goals you have always dreamed of and are finally ready to achieve. Whatever you are seeking, my goal is to help you lighten your load and provide you with the peace you deserve.

I know many of us are carrying the weight of more. More decisions, more economic pressure, more financial uncertainty, and more of the fatigue that comes with it. This is one of the main reasons I'm writing this book. I've lived through the burnout, the exhaustion, and the noise, and I've also experienced the freedom and power that the right kind of less gives us. Know that you *can* create a better way forward and a life you truly deserve.

Beyond the valuable rewards of less, the most important thing I hope you take away in the pages ahead is the clarity it will give you. We live in a complex world. And in times like these, we need clarity more than ever. We must deliberately focus on *less* to experience and make room for the right *more*. In making this shift toward less, we truly allow ourselves to get clear on what matters. That is the clarity that this book can give you.

## LESS OVER MORE: KEY INSIGHTS

- **Less creates more** by opening space for opportunities, growth, and peace.
- **Our programming** from birth to age seven shapes our beliefs about scarcity versus abundance.
- **The spiritual component** is that we cocreate with the universe but must be ready to receive.
- **Thoughts drive all results,** so changing your mindset is fundamental to success.

# PART I

# THE ILLUSION OF MORE

# CHAPTER 1
# THE MYTH OF MORE, MORE, AND MORE

## WHEN DID MORE BECOME THE MEASURE?

Outperforming. Outearning. Outpacing. Outspending. And outworking others as the yardstick to measure success. The race to more has become normalized, and it may be the biggest lie we have ever learned. Yet when did this myth of *more* being the path to success in life and business begin?

Daily, we are inundated with the myth of more via social media, marketing, lifestyles, and the ever-present comparison game. Chasing more often dilutes your true purpose, pulling you away from the goals that matter most. The real question that we will explore is, what if the world has it wrong and we have blindly walked into this way of existing? What if more is a myth?

We are conditioned to think more will ease stress while bringing happiness, contentment, peace, and joy to our lives. However, it does the opposite. More creates stress, frustration, anger, resentment, fear, guilt, and hurt.

Here's something you might consider: As you reflect on your life, your family, business, friendships, and possessions, what emotions do you have toward the "more" situation you may have created?

## THE DESTINATION ADDICTION

We often tell ourselves that our drive for more is okay because "one day" we will have it all—the job, the house, the car, the life, and so forth. The reality is you are not enjoying the journey or the present moment you are in. You are experiencing Destination Addiction, which is fueled by *more*. Coined by Robert Holden, PhD, it's the belief that when you get something else (more), you will finally be happy.

You may have heard yourself saying one of these phrases:

"When I get the promotion . . ."
"When I get the big house . . ."
"When I get the vacation home . . ."
"When I meet the right person . . ."
"When I can buy a bigger diamond . . ."

These are a sign of Destination Addiction—addiction to *more*. If this is you, know that you may be missing out on the present moment. Your journey has become about your happiness existing elsewhere, not where you are right now.

## MY CORPORATE HAMSTER WHEEL

I lived on the Destination Addiction Hamster Wheel for years. When I reflect on my early days in my corporate career, I see I was *in it* big time! In my sophomore year of college, I decided that I wanted to work in the hospitality industry. I took a job at Marriott Hotels at their Worldwide Reservation Center as a reservation agent. I was surrounded by others in the same role as me, yet I was also surrounded by supervisors, managers, directors, and executives. I saw them all in their suits, expensive shoes, and important positions. I assumed they all lived bigger lives than me, as they were making way more money than me. Then the "more" lightbulb turned on: I would realize happiness when I got promoted and became one of "them."

I did everything I could to become a supervisor as quickly as possible. I volunteered for focus groups, both as a participant and a moderator as needed, picked up shifts when needed, anything. I achieved that goal, but I wasn't in my new supervisor role for a week before I became focused on getting a management position. I repeated the more game over and over. Eventually I did hold many executive leadership roles with Marriott.

What finally happened is I ran out of "next destinations."

I found myself with the titles, salary, bonus, fancy suits, house, car, vacations, and lots of nonessential stuff, but I also found myself stressed, frustrated, exhausted, and resentful. I had no life outside of work (my choice) and felt completely spent. The fancy car, a BMW convertible, I barely drove except to and from work. The house served as a place to crash at night; the expensive suits never saw much use outside of work or a work event.

If this sounds all too familiar, you may be living in More!

## HOW DID THIS HAPPEN?

Gradually and then suddenly—one of my favorite concepts learned from Ernest Hemingway's 1926 novel *The Sun Also Rises*. Gradually, it was an item or two, and suddenly it was a house *full* of nonessential items.

My experience (and potentially yours) supports the concept of more being a lie. The belief that accumulating more—be it material possessions, commitments, or information—will lead to happiness often results in stress and overwhelm. This pursuit can create a cycle of dissatisfaction, as you constantly chase more without ever feeling fulfilled. To say I was stressed and overwhelmed was an understatement. I do believe I accumulated so many things with the intention of them bringing me happiness. Sadly, over time, it did the complete opposite.

## FROM SEARS TO STATUS SYMBOLS

Coming from a very modest upbringing by first-generation American parents, I saw a different way of living than anything I later experienced in my corporate environment. We were raised with "enough," and the things we had were necessity, not luxury. To prepare for the school year, we went to JC Penney or Sears to get the basics and nothing more. I remember dreading those trips to buy my school clothes. Nothing about it was fun! I could sense my mom's stress, as she had a limited budget to work with. I also knew I was going to leave the mall disappointed, as I didn't get to buy anything just because it looked good; it all had to serve a purpose and last a *long* time.

For my parents, it was truly all about the function, price, and durability of the clothing. I watched my mom find the pants that would wear the longest and last the entire school year, made from thick denim with built-in knee patches. I *hated* these pants. It has been decades since I put on a pair of pants like that, yet I can still feel the stiffness of the material and the outline of the inside patch. It was like walking with cardboard around my legs, with the patch irritating the skin on my knees.

Then, once I entered young adulthood and my new corporate environment, for the first time I saw nice homes and cars, designer suits and handbags, gorgeous shoes, and more. I witnessed people making salaries I had never even thought possible. It appeared that this was because they worked hard, outperformed their peers, and were always doing more. I was hooked and ready to give it my all.

## THE STAGGERING STATISTICS OF MORE

We have slipped so far into the "more equation" as a society that we are fueled with consumption to the point of excess. We have so much "stuff" that we need to rent storage units to hold the things that no longer fit in our homes:

**Storage and Consumption Statistics**

- $38 billion is spent annually on self-storage.[1]
- This statistic is growing annually and is estimated to be $72 billion by 2029.[2]
- There are 23 million storage units in the United States.[3]
- The average American throws out 81 pounds of clothing each year.[4]
- Americans give away about 12 million tons of furniture each year.[5]

**The Modern American Home**

- There are 300,000 items in the average American home.[6]
- Home size has grown by 150% since 1980.[7]
- According to British research, the average 10-year-old owns 238 toys but only plays with 12 daily.[8]
- The United States is home to 3.1% of the world's children, who own 40% of the toys consumed globally.[9]
- The average American woman owns 30 outfits, one for every day of the month (in 1930, that number was 9).[10]

**Spending Patterns**

- Americans spend more on shoes, jewelry, and watches ($100 billion annually) than on higher education.[11]
- The average American wastes $18,000 per year on these nonessentials.[12]

This is one of those times that you become numb to reality because you are *in* it. It is hard to be an observer when it just becomes a habit and the norm. Is it time to rethink the pursuit of more?

## THE HIDDEN COSTS OF MORE

To further dive into "more is a lie," consider this affliction extending beyond material accumulation and into various other contexts, each holding a deeper implication for your well-being and views on society. More can be misleading or detrimental . . . and even disastrous.

Here are eight lies of more:

### Lie #1. Burnout and Overcommitment

The thought that taking on more responsibilities equates to productivity or success, be it at work, in social commitments, or on personal projects, can lead to burnout. Stretching yourself too thin can diminish your overall performance and satisfaction, resulting in lower quality of work, relationships, and personal health.

### Lie #2. False Sense of Security

The accumulation of wealth, possessions, or status can create a superficial sense of security. Relying on these external validations can lead to vulnerability, as they can be taken away or lost. Your true security stems from self-awareness and authentic relationships, not from material possessions or nonessential items.

### Lie #3. The Comparison Game

Comparison is often called the thief of joy. This constant chase of more can fuel a culture of comparison, where you gauge your worth against others'. This not only causes feelings of inadequacy or being less than but also creates envy and competition . . . ultimately distracting you from any sense of community and connection.

**Lie #4. Information Overload**

We are flooded with information and data, driving us to information overload. This overload can cause serious decision paralysis and take your focus away from what is truly important. Quality of information is more important than quantity of information.

**Lie #5. Destination Addiction**

Our compulsion for more can have us constantly chasing future goals, possessions, or the next best thing, causing us to ignore the present moment. When we ignore the present, it dramatically dampens our appreciation for what we have. Until you are grateful for what you have, it is hard for the universe to give you more.

**Lie #6. Artificial Relationships**

Creating a larger social circle or focusing on more influential connections can result in superficial relationships. Again, favoring quantity over quality hinders meaningful connections. You are so distracted with the quantity that you miss out on the true meaningful relationships that are right in front of you!

**Lie #7. Environmental Impact**

What happens to all the "stuff" you collect that you (or your survivors) eventually will dispose of? Offloading this excess may damage the environment when it goes into landfills, harming generations to come.

**Lie #8. Mental Health Impact**

The constant pressure to have more, whether in personal achievements, career advancement, or social status, can have massive mental health implications, including anxiety, depression, and lower self-esteem (via comparison).

## LESS AS ABUNDANCE

What would less look like if it were abundance? Would you see it as a *win* versus a sacrifice? How would it feel? What impact would it truly have on your life and business? How would others still in the more zone receive it?

What does less look like when based in scarcity? Scarcity is the belief that resources—be they financial, social, or emotional—are limited. You focus on what you lack versus what you have. While many live in the space of scarcity, know it is a choice, as is living in less. Less is an intentional elimination of more, which in this case can be work tasks, essential and nonessential items, chores, and the like.

## JOY VERSUS HAPPINESS: UNDERSTANDING THE DIFFERENCE

"The more we have, the happier we are" is a common myth. The truth is that joy is the true driver of peace and enjoyment—not things.

Happiness is driven by external circumstances or happenstance. Those moments are fleeting and create a swing of emotions: the initial rush, the level-off, and then the letdown.

I remember the first time I bought myself a *new* car. It was a blue Camaro. I was that guy who *loved* cars. I was always looking at different options and knew more about the car makes and models than nearly anything else in life.

As I walked into H+H Chevrolet in Omaha, Nebraska, to make the purchase, my heart was racing and the smile on my face ran from ear to ear. I felt like I was watching myself and not in my body any longer. I worked hard to get the best deal possible and a monthly payment that I could afford. This was my first *big* decision and *big* purchase. I signed the contract and could *not* wait to get the keys and drive off.

Then the moment came and they pulled the car around, shiny and clean and ready for me, its new owner! I sat in the car, adjusted the seats, mirror, and all-important radio, then took in the sights, smells, and sounds of my new ride. As I put it in reverse to drive off the lot, the happy hormones were *rushing*.

For weeks, possibly even months, every time I walked out to my car, I had a euphoric feeling. Then at some point, probably after a few car payments, I remember it suddenly just felt like . . . a car.

I found myself thinking, *Is this worth it?* The happy factor wore off, and though it was truly still a great car, it no longer provided the same rush it had not so long ago. That is typically what happens with external factors—they do not endure.

At the same time, happiness can numb pain, yet it also can create it. That "hit" of happy hormones feels so good that it may compel us to create it over and over. This is where the danger of "consumption and collection" can enter. That rush and euphoria of making a purchase or collecting an item is undeniably a great feeling. Yet when the "high" wears off, you are often left with buyer's remorse or disappointment. Then your brain tricks you to go do it again—surely this time it will make a difference! So, you go secure something else and get to feel the feel-good hormone release again . . . and then, the letdown.

The roller coaster of happy can be one of the drivers of *more*.

Unlike happiness, joy is internal and can be called upon at any time. It comes from a sense of purpose and meaning. It is an emotion and a state of mind. Sitting in gratitude and appreciation is a form of joy. Embracing your achievements, reaching a goal or fulfilling a dream, both conjure joy.

## A PERSONAL REVELATION: THE MOVING EXPERIENCE

Much like my experience earlier in my corporate life, the "more" myth appeared again when it was exposed during our move to Santa Fe. Reagan and I were moving out of one of our homes that we'd lived in for many years. It was during a time in our lives when we were immersed in more. We'd finally been able to afford what we wanted and when we wanted it. No more saving and scrimping to collect things. Consequently, our house filled with items, yet we continued to bring in more and more.

So, when we moved, we found closets, drawers, and attic space full of those things that once made us happy for a brief moment. As we began the sorting, tossing, and packing process, we set aside a garage full of "stuff" to donate. Many of the items we hadn't seen in years and honestly forgot that we even had purchased. The shine had worn off, and we'd put them away in a box to "use later."

Multiple truckloads of donations to a very happy local charity later, we had cleared out the space. We both noticed that we had zero emotion around the items. At one point, we played the "How much did we spend on this stuff?" game, but we stopped ourselves when we hit a disturbing number!

## THE SANTA FE TRANSFORMATION

One of our intentional choices of less came when we moved to Santa Fe and were furnishing our new home. We were moving the contents of both our primary home and our secondary home, also full of stuff.

(We had sold our second home years prior to this move and had done the dreaded "placing our stuff in a storage unit for future use" routine.)

Once in Santa Fe, we had the contents of both households delivered in large, box shipping containers. What we had spent thousands of dollars on storing meant absolutely nothing to us years later. In fact, we then disposed of (donated and tossed) more than 90% of the things we'd held in storage.

It was overwhelming to sort through the excess we had stashed in each box and each crate. It was truly a sea of cardboard full of things that we hadn't seen in *years*! Things that at the time we viewed as irreplaceable and had held some meaning for us. We quickly realized that all we'd held near and dear was truly just extra stuff—noise, if you will. At one point, while we were both opening up boxes, we lost sight of each other in the massive mountain of cardboard. I had to search to find Reagan; when I did, we looked at each other and just laughed.

We came to the same conclusion simultaneously: that holding onto the "more" was not only a financial waste but also taking up precious space in our lives. At that moment, our unspoken conversation was shared. We knew all the stuff was truly blocking us, and we were carrying forward the life that we'd wished and intended to leave behind. How could we start fresh with all of the extra? How could we build our dream life if we were carrying forward our old visions? We knew it was time to edit and delete.

In an instant, we were unburdened with forcing the "more" into our new life while unknowingly creating a spiritual boundary of less. This allowed us to experience new boundaries in our home life and feel the relief associated with them. That decision to leave more space empty than full allowed us to let things come to us on our new journey.

As we started in our new life of "less," the most amazing pieces of art and unique artifacts magically appeared. Had we filled the house with the "more" stuff, we never would have looked at anything else—we'd have ignored the blessings we found, as there wouldn't have been the space for it.

As with life and work, you must create the space to welcome and nurture new opportunities. In our new life, we were extremely particular as to what we would bring into our lives. It was no longer about collecting more; now it was about having the right amount of less that allowed for true joy.

Less helps reduce distractions, be they material items, digital clutter, or excessive commitments. Less fosters mental clarity and enhances focus, allowing you to dedicate more time and energy to what truly matters. Less clears the path to peace and success.

Are you ready to clear your path? If so, peace and success are just around the corner waiting for you.

If being on the "more" hamster wheel feels relatable, great news: Now you get to decide whether you will remain on it or step off. Plus, you get to step off to less or to a fitting more. This one decision can be the thing that allows you to experience true joy versus fleeting happiness. To be present and to be joyful with where you are versus postponing your joy until your next destination.

Let yourself sit in that possibility for a moment. What emotions are you feeling? Relief? Joy? Peace? Stillness? What impact can this one decision have on your current business, relationships, or life? Allow yourself to "dream" about it and lean into the peace that comes from this possibility. Know that if you can imagine it, you can become it.

## LESS OVER MORE: KEY INSIGHTS

- **Destination Addiction** is about constantly chasing the next thing, which prevents present-moment happiness.
- **Americans spend** $1.2 trillion annually on nonessential goods.
- **The average American home** contains 300,000 items.
- **Joy versus Happiness:** Joy is internal and sustainable; happiness is external and fleeting.
- **Moving toward less:** Helps reduce distractions be it material, digital, or commitments.
- **Pursuing more often leads to** stress, overwhelm, and decreased life satisfaction.

# CHAPTER 2

# HOW THE WORLD SHAPED YOUR BELIEFS

Having embraced the fact that my thoughts and beliefs shape the life I live and the results I get, I started to put the pieces together and understand why I was having the experiences I'd had—especially why I was haunted by the experience of "just enough" or "barely enough." I was raised in my parents' first home, along with my two sisters. It was a small house, three bedrooms and one bath, and it measured 912 square feet. There was no central air conditioning, just a window unit in the living room where we would camp out on the hot summer nights. My dad, a pharmacist, and my mom, a nurse, were living the American Dream. For first-generation Americans, having your own home, respected professions with degrees, three kids, and two cars was pretty impressive.

When I was about two years old, my dad bought into a small chain of drug stores, which I'm certain was a scary decision for him and my mom. Mom quit her nursing job when my oldest sister was born and helped my dad run the family business. I never witnessed them experiencing abundance or sharing that possibility with our family. Talking about money was taboo in our home and never discussed openly. We never had the latest and greatest, yet we had just enough. It was made clear to us that when we would get clothing, toys, or the like, we were to take care of them. If we broke or lost something, it would not be replaced.

## THE ENVIRONMENT OF SCARCITY

It wasn't until I was looking back as an adult that I realized I'd been raised in an environment of scarcity. We never did much as a family. We stayed in our house, ate 98% of our meals at home, and didn't take vacations. Mom packed homemade lunches for us to take to school and my dad to take to work. I recall only going to two movies as a child, as they were considered luxuries. There was always food in the refrigerator but no bags of chips or other snacks in the house. We had what we needed and not much more, in the confines of our little home.

Things were "okay" until I was around five or six years old, when the neighborhood became dangerous to live in. At times, my dad would have us get on the ground for fear of stray bullets from gunshots outside. My parents were truly forced to move for our safety. What was interesting is, we moved as *far* away from our old home as possible. The new house was much larger and fit the family better. Yet, as you can imagine, my parents' beliefs and thoughts from our old house followed us to the new one. Their scarcity mindset continued, amplified by buying a home that was significantly larger and pricier than their previous home. They were forced to make a decision from the position of scarcity and, to be honest, I'm surprised they made such a bold move. I believe the pain of staying in a dangerous situation drove their decision by forcing them to move toward pleasure (safety).

Ultimately, my beliefs were formed around this "just enough" scarcity of pursuing the basics and nothing more. I didn't know any different, and as I grew into young adulthood, those familiar beliefs came with me, impacting many of my decisions. I didn't join any sports or school clubs, as they cost money, and in my heart I knew we couldn't or wouldn't spend on them. I silenced my desires for the latest and greatest fads and didn't ask for anything that wasn't a necessity.

Later, during a conversation with some friends, we were discussing our families and our experiences during our very formative years. In that chat, I realized that there was an element of stress that seemed ever present in my childhood house, like a constant background buzz regardless of what was happening. I believe it was created by my parents' programming and beliefs around scarcity and fear. Being children of the Depression during their formative first eight or nine years, they witnessed food rationing, furniture repossessions, and days of truly having not enough. Suddenly I realized why they had the beliefs they had and how the world shaped their experiences.

## THE OMAHA INFLUENCE

Growing up in Omaha, Nebraska, in the 1960s and 1970s was amazing in many ways, and in others, limiting. I always questioned why my immigrant grandparents selected Omaha, passing through great cities like NYC or Chicago. Later in life, I learned that Omaha was chosen for them because of their employment opportunities with the railroad. You went to where the job was and were happy to have the job, regardless of the city.

Omaha was a city of solid, pull-yourself-up, hard-work-ethic Midwestern people. It was still a small town but on the cusp of growing. It was a simple town; people had what they needed, worked hard, and kept to themselves. What I didn't realize for years is that many of the "hard workers" were extremely wealthy. You see, you didn't talk about that in Omaha. I didn't know any wealthy people (well, I did, I just didn't know it), so my beliefs were not those of abundance. I didn't see anyone living a big life. I only saw people working really hard, living modest lives. No fancy cars, no mansions, just average and ordinary lives. Ultimately this formed my beliefs that you simply work hard, accept the norm, and settle in for the long haul—and wealthy people *only* existed on TV and in Hollywood!

## THE PROGRAMMING PROCESS: YOUR MENTAL SMARTPHONE

It wasn't until I was exposed to Neuro-Linguistic Programming (NLP) in 2010 that I learned how our beliefs and thoughts are formed and imprinted heavily from birth to age seven. Those beliefs drive our decisions and become the framework of our lives. Now, in our current environment of external influence through social media and the internet, we are exposed to a world outside of our immediate family, inner circle, state, and country. This exposure can challenge your existing beliefs and instill new ones.

The best example I can give regarding the beliefs you are exposed to and the influence the world has on them is to think about a newborn being just like a new smartphone. The smartphone is delivered to you with only the programs it needs to function. Like a new phone, newborns know the basics: how to breathe, circulate blood, nurse, cry, and so on. And when babies are delivered, they, like a smartphone, start to download needed apps that will make their lives better. Suddenly, the purity of that smartphone is gone, and you have multiple programs running at all times all with different benefits and value. This is the same as when a newborn is receiving programming from their family, the news, the internet, television shows, cartoons, and so forth. One by one, these influences are creating programs inside of the newborn's world, shaping their beliefs.

## MY COLLEGE AWAKENING

For me, I distinctly remember when my beliefs were challenged the most: when I went off to college and began living on campus, away from home. My new circle of friends there began showing me a new set of beliefs. In those moments, I realized there was a different way. It was the first time I met parents who believed their kid could become famous, successful, wealthy, and powerful. Who allowed their kids to think bigger and outside of their immediate circle. It really jostled my beliefs.

At first, this way of living felt fake or like a con job. It couldn't have seemed further from my truth and my ingrained beliefs. If I'm totally honest, I felt like I needed to distance myself from it, as it was so odd to me. However, something about it oddly felt good. As I found myself spending more time with families who thought differently than mine, their reality felt less "scammy" and more authentic. I started to see glimmers of a different way. I didn't ditch my belief system yet, but I began feeling the pull to different beliefs and the possibility of "more." The big house, the nice cars, the luxury goods—they all seemed to be making the other families happy, less stressed, and carefree in their experiences.

I started to truly enjoy the energy and sense of possibility I felt when I spent time with other families and friends. For the first time, I not only wanted more, but I actually believed it was possible—and possible for me. Oddly, whenever I returned home to visit, what once felt normal now seemed foreign and small. The beliefs I was raised with regarding a bigger life, success, and career opportunities no longer fit, and the contrast between my parents' way and the new way I was experiencing was startling. That sense of disconnection from my old beliefs was jarring—but it also marked a turning point. By the end of college and early in my professional career, the pull toward more was undeniable and fully in motion.

I began watching what successful people were doing. What they were buying, spending time doing, wearing, driving, saying, creating, and doing professionally, along with how they were acting. From the outside looking in, it appeared as if they were happy and enjoying their journeys. Over time, I found myself emulating them all too well and slid into the cycle of more, believing it was the "way."

Oddly, this drive to more is very much an "inner" game, yet it is an external demonstration! I was so internally driven to play the game at a very high level that, to prove my commitment and obsession with more, I had to show the world my success. Suddenly the car I drove was more important to me than being kind. Doing whatever it took to get to the next level was more critical than doing the right thing. I had to prove that I was succeeding by showing everyone my wins.

This external validation can be misunderstood. For example, my parents were so proud of me for every promotion I received or for the fun cars I was able to buy, yet they didn't truly know my hidden agenda. So, I was rewarded through recognition by my family and friends, and it further fueled my more mentality. In addition, my employer was beyond thrilled at the level in which I was showing up. Crushing it and destroying my competition. Receiving "awards" and public praise. All of it fueled my drive and added another category of more: more awards, more acknowledgment, and more "look at me" external validation!

## THE BURNOUT BREAKING POINT

More is addictive and exhausting. It leads to burnout. And this cycle of addictive behavior and exhaustion can last for years, even decades. Eventually, it can break us. We all have different moments in life when we realize more is suffocating. You simply do not have the capacity for one more thing. "More" becomes the proverbial straw that breaks the camel's back. You arrive at the point where you know "more" will make you miserable. You are already starting to feel the harm, and something in you awakens and realizes, you just can't.

## THE HOOD TEST

I distinctly remember my "moment" when I was in the hotel industry. I had left Marriott and was working for a boutique-hotel company in Dallas. We were a small chain of eight hotels, and the goal was to be a five-star player in the industry. It sounded like the perfect fit for me and was filling my quest for more. I had a title that I hadn't held before in a full-service hotel, the pay was amazing, the benefits were equal to my previous position, and it was at a hotel that I had always admired as a guest. This new salary and position were another whack at more and would allow me to do and have more (car, pool, home, travel, etc.).

The reality was that the executive team at the hotel had already been conditioned and exposed to a certain set of beliefs by the general manager. These included the belief that we gave up our lives for the hotel, and the hotel was our primary focus in life and business. The hours I was working were wild, yet they were the norm at this company! I was responsible for all departments in the hotel except banquets and sales. What this meant was arriving at 5 AM to ensure operations were set for the day and not leaving until 11-ish PM to ensure the evening crew was performing. Determined to succeed, I caved and gave in to the norm. More hours, more bonuses, and more recognition.

Then one day, I had been at work for a few hours when I was outside talking to the valet team. I noticed my general manager pulling into the parking lot. Instead of walking toward the entrance to the hotel, he went over to my car, placed his hand on the hood, and stood there momentarily.

Curious as to what he was doing, I turned to the bell captain and asked if he knew what was going on. He replied, "He does this every day. He is testing the heat of the hood of your car to estimate how long you have been at the hotel working."

I immediately felt anger and distrust. Thoughts started flooding my mind. *What the what* is he doing? I get here at 5 AM nearly every morning and ensure that the *entire* hotel is functioning so he can breeze in at 7 AM and walk into a functioning hotel. In a flash, I realized this was his version of leadership: suspicion and distrust. This was his true measurement of my value—his belief in what it meant to be successful in his presence. How long I had been at the hotel versus the quality of work I was doing. Not my work ethic, not the way I went above and beyond for the hotel and our guests. Just assessing if he was getting "more out of me" every day from the temperature of my car?

You know the line about the straw and the camel? Well, that was it—the defining moment when I realized, enough! I saw how my beliefs were completely out of alignment with his. That everything I learned from the best in the industry, Marriott, was not respected at this company and I had fallen away from them. I had been positioned for a promotion to general manager. I'd seen this as an opportunity to rise in the ranks and accumulate more influence and power. While it was a position of power, I now realized it wasn't the kind of power I cared about any longer. This was my *first* experience of realizing that if I got any "more," I would have snapped or been miserable, and that I was chasing the "wrong more." Instead, I resigned from the hotel industry and decided to choose less!

## THE CULTURAL DRIVERS OF MORE

So why, *why* would we allow "more" to be so addictive and seductive and possibly violate our core beliefs? We know the obvious consumption reasons, how it might be the norm in America and other rich countries, yet there has to be something deeper. What is driving this?

Part of the consumption equation is to participate in our "Bigger, Better, Faster" world. A world of instant gratification is upon us. We want it *now*. We want more than our peers; we want it to be better, and we want to have it faster!

Think about how Amazon fulfills that itch. When we lived in Austin, Texas, by an Amazon distribution center, we could have an order to us in less than two hours—*two*! Worst case, we had to wait for the following day. Also, the products made available to us via Amazon or other manufacturers are focused on the bigger and better part of the equation. Each year's model or product claims to outperform the previous year's and is marketed to us as "bigger and better." The harsh reality is, much of it is bigger, yet the quality—the "better"—is questionable.

## THE APPLE EXAMPLE

Being an Apple fan, all my technology is Apple, from iPhone to iPad to the MacBook Pro on which I am writing this book. Rarely does my Apple product wear out and need to be replaced. These replacements would come from the "more" and "better" space. The new phone has a better camera. It "looks" different from the previous model. It has more speed. And so forth. The reality is, my current phone is working beautifully, yet I want what is perceived as bigger, better, and faster. Again, the external validation for the inner game we are playing can compel us to do things that are not necessary! Truly, having the latest version of the iPhone for no other reason than for the world to see that I could afford it, or that I was so important that I needed it, could stoke my addiction to consuming.

A study by Roy Baumeister specifies a framework of impulse buying as a failure of self-regulation driven by instant gratification, emotional states, and external stimuli.[13] This makes complete sense when it comes to many of our purchases, my Apple products included. Something catches my attention, and without much thought, the item is placed in my cart, and I buy and feel a rush of instant gratification about my purchase.

## THE STANFORD MARSHMALLOW EXPERIMENT

In 1972, a great experiment regarding delayed gratification was conducted. The Stanford Marshmallow Experiment involved a group of preschoolers who were offered a marshmallow and told they could have a second one *if* they waited a certain amount of time (15 minutes) without eating the first.[14]

- **The results:** Children who were able to resist the temptation and wait for the second marshmallow tended to have better academic outcomes, higher SAT scores, and better emotional coping skills later in life.
- **Key insight:** Direct correlation between delayed gratification and self-control in achieving long-term success.
- **Follow-up:** Years later, participants who displayed better self-control in the test tended to have more positive outcomes in various areas of their lives.

Instant gratification can cause stress in the "more" world. The compulsion for *now* will often outweigh the financial implications. Purchasing a big-ticket item that you may not truly be able to afford, just to fulfill your more consumption state, can and will lead to financial stress. The temporary feeling of happiness will happen, yet underlying it will be stress, fear, or anxiety about paying for the item.

## AMERICAN CONSUMPTION VERSUS THE WORLD

Americans have a higher rate of consumption than most other countries. Our spending habits in obtaining more leave other countries perplexed. In America, we live to work! The average American takes about 11 days off per year.[15] Our European counterparts are required to take around 20 days annually.[16] Americans are less likely to take all their vacation days and feel that they "can't" take time away from their jobs.[17]

We also consume more than our European counterparts. Americans buy more goods annually than any other country. Tracked consumption per capita grew to 65% in the United States between 1990 and 2015, while in Europe it grew only 35%.[18]

## CONSUMPTION FOR THE SAKE OF BIGGER AND BETTER—THOUGHTS TO PONDER

Pause and get honest with yourself. Is there an area of your life, career, or relationship in which, more often than not, you are on a quest for the next best thing? The bigger or better version of what you already have? One way to identify this is, what are you disposing of or giving away that is still functional, yet you opted to replace it with the next best thing? Technology? Clothing or designer bags? Cars? *Your spouse?*

When we get the urge to replace, the key question to ask yourself is, "Does the existing item I am replacing still function and have value?" Will someone else find value in it? If the answer is yes, you may be unconsciously sliding into the bigger and better way.

## THE DANISH ALTERNATIVE: *HYGGE*

Many of us are at the precipice of an awakening or an awareness. More is starting to lose its shine! No longer can it motivate or drive us like it used to. This process may be a rapid, complete departure from more to less, or a gradual change. The self-imposed pressure cooker can feel good at first and last quite a long time. Yet for some of us, the lid finally blows off, and we are faced with doing something different. Perhaps we are connecting to our core beliefs again.

Maybe we could take a lesson from our Danish friends. They have a way of life that allows for an attachment to what they feel is most important, bringing them a feeling of warmth, coziness, and shared moments of happiness. This word and philosophy, *hygge*, has captured world attention. At its root, *hygge* evolved as a survival strategy during Denmark's long, dark, cold winters. Yet even when removed from the harsh climate where it was born, *hygge* has its place in the world.

*Hygge* is based on several key elements:

- **Ambiance and Lighting:** *Hygge* thrives in the glow of gentle, diffused lighting. It involves a lot of candles, as the flickering flames provide a sense of warmth and a soothing ambiance that is instantly comforting.
- **Clothing:** While no specific dress code is involved, think of the comfort of your softest sweater or favorite joggers. The ones you turn to when you want to feel cozy and comfortable.

- **Food and Drink:** Culinary delights play a big role in *hygge*. It is not about abundance but heartwarming simplicity. A mug of cocoa, freshly baked desserts or pastries, or a warm bowl of stew. It is not only the taste of the food that creates *hygge* but also its aroma.
- **Togetherness:** One of the most profound aspects of *hygge* is the focus on social connections. Cherishing the company of family and friends. Engaging in profound conversations. Even spending time together in simple silence.

A lot of lessons can be learned from our Danish friends. One important element to consider is that *hygge* is on the "less" side and allows the space for peace, joy, and stress release. It is a great example of how less can provide more—more peace, more clarity, more connectedness and love.

## MY PERSONAL CAVE: FINDING LESS BEFORE I KNEW IT

Without ever knowing what *hygge* was, and before our Santa Fe evolution, we had a second home at a lake outside of Dallas. This lake community was primarily weekend homes with a small percentage of full-time residents. Nearly every Wednesday, I would head to the lake to "cave." To me, caving is spending time alone to recharge. I called it "unplugging to plug in." I unplugged from the "more" of life and work to plug into solitude and peace. It was a much-needed respite.

To say it was quiet at the lake during the week is an understatement. I remember pulling into our neighborhood and it being extremely dark, no lights on in the homes and no sign of "life." There were no street lights, no merchants; just a dark night sky with stars lighting the way.

The closer I got to our house, the more stress I could feel leaving my body, anticipating entry to our space of comfort.

This house was completely different from any house we had owned. It had a definite lake vibe to it—a place where you wanted to kick your shoes off, put on your comfy clothes or shorts, and curl up on the sofa. It also had a great fireplace that helped create a mood of calm during the winter. The furniture was designed for relaxation, with the best napping sofa and chairs. The house also had a distinctive, amazing smell, from sitting directly on 180 feet of open water. Along with the clear skies, the stars, and the moon, the setting was amazing.

On occasion, I'd bring a friend with me, and he, much like me, was perfectly fine with the silence. Many nights, we'd grab a bite to eat and each quietly enjoy our meals. No need to talk, no need for the television. Wednesdays and the lake house became my private sanctuary. What was amazing to me is that on weekends, this same house was full of friends and family and activity. Far from a quiet place to cave! Yet full of the spirit of love and fun.

Does the simplicity of less catch your attention? Are you realizing that you have become numb to your current state of more? Are you at your breaking point with more? Is it bubbling up? The good news, you don't have to wait for the straw that breaks the camel's back. You can make a choice now. A choice now of delayed gratification, only replacing items that are worn out versus bigger and better for the sake of bigger and better. Is it time to let go of generational programming that will set you free to live the life you truly desire? Get ready to learn how less can help you create the most abundant and rewarding business and life.

## LESS OVER MORE: KEY INSIGHTS

- **Your brain seeks data** that confirms your existing beliefs (confirmation bias).
- **The "attention economy" capitalizes** on our focus and drives consumption.
- **Breaking generational programming** requires conscious effort and commitment.
- ***Hygge* is a Danish concept** that shows how less can create more peace and connection.

## CHAPTER 3

# GOING AGAINST THE NORM OF MORE

Going against the norm seems to be the underlying theme of my life, except when it came to embracing the "norm of more." From a young age, I felt out of place or uncomfortable following the norm. In my family, the norm was to be a devout Catholic, contribute to society through work and charity, and accept what was given. Oh, and a career in the medical profession wouldn't hurt your cause.

While I chose to contribute in my own way, I was the only one in our family who was not in some medical profession. My dad was a pharmacist, my mom was a nurse, my oldest sister has a doctorate in pharmacy, and my middle sister is a nurse. My siblings are both incredibly intelligent and crushed it in high school and at university. And me? Hey, if I got a C and could check it off my list, all was good.

I typically felt on the fringe of the norm in most areas of my life, from my friends to my religious beliefs, aspirations, and more. I ended up withdrawing a bit, as it felt uncomfortable to be on the "outside" looking in. Toss in not fitting into the norm of the Midwest values and ideals. Being gay at a time when it wasn't "okay" to be gay, *the norm felt very foreign to me.* I was different. My sense of the norm would be different. And logically, that was fine by me, yet it took an emotional toll. Plus, I was figuring this all out on my own, as I had no adult I could turn to for guidance. Still, I knew in my gut that my path would be unlike others'.

Maybe your norm and your path are different as well, for whatever reason: different values, politics, beliefs, preferences, or a pull in a new career direction—whatever it may be. Have you made peace with the path you've chosen? Acknowledged your path may be very different from everyone else's? Accepted its uniqueness and embraced the discomfort of others not understanding or respecting your path? Embraced that, like your fingerprint, your journey may be one of a kind?

Maybe you are like I was, and know in your gut your path is different, even though you are not certain of what your norm is right now or even for your life ahead. Trust the process and know we will get there.

## FINDING MY PLACE IN MORE

When I came across the American culture of "more," I embraced it without hesitation. For the first time, I felt in step with the majority—a place where I finally belonged.

Yet after decades of living in the norm of more when it came to work and life, a time came when I knew it was no longer for me. I started to feel the impact of the full range of stress that is connected to more, from the pressures in my corporate career to the self-imposed pressures in my career as an entrepreneur. Moving beyond the norm feels like letting go of the familiar. It may be painful but it's liberating. Going after the norm *you* want will set you free.

Moving beyond the norm requires you to embrace letting go of what feels familiar and comfortable. Letting go of what you know and trusting that there is something else out there. It is much like one of my favorite quotes:

> We must be willing to get rid of the life we've planned, so as to have the life that is waiting for us.
>
> —Joseph Campbell[19]

Will you step into the unknown? Is it your time to take that leap of faith? Will you honor your gut and trust it when it is making you aware that something is off and that something must change, even if you don't know 100% what that change will be?

## THE CEILING OF MORE

I can't explain it. One day, when you have "everything," yet you no longer have emotion toward it, you may have hit the ceiling of more. For me, I was just going through the motions. Buying more, doing more, overextending myself with projects, clients, and commitments. Living in fear that if I ever said "No!" to a work opportunity, it would be a sign of weakness to the outside world. Worse yet, what if an opportunity I turned down was presented to my competition and they said yes . . . *eek!*

When I made the decision to leave "more" behind and step out, a lot of old insecurities came back to me. Will I be ignored? Will I fail? Will I feel on the "outside" looking in and feel invisible? Will I lose it all?

This journey against the norm has a lot of elements and feelings that you must be ready to experience. I was not.

## CONSPICUOUS CONSUMPTION AND THE ATTENTION ECONOMY

I will admit, while living in the more, it felt good. It came with a lot of highs—a euphoric feeling when I accomplished something big, like a new job, car, or investment. Much of the time, I did not "need" this more, yet it was part of my habits and programming.

Let's face it, *we live in a capitalistic culture that thrives on consumers' dissatisfaction.* That dissatisfaction can drive us to find the "next best thing." Think about how many "new models" are introduced by major brands: cars, electronics, smartphones. For me, if I owned a car and a new model came out, without hesitation I was at the dealership trading the "old" model in, regardless of how long I'd owned the previous model or its condition. Our culture truly defines success through work promotions, the latest and greatest, and the accumulation of nonessential items. Toss in social media influencers likewise under a heavy influence of more and it truly just fuels the fire. Consider the trend of GRWM (get ready with me) videos that feature expensive products to create the desire for more and stoke FOMO (fear of missing out). We feel compelled to keep up with trends and outpace other's success and consumption. As Herbert A. Simon wrote in the 1960s, "we are 'the attention economy.'" Human attention is now treated as a valuable and scarce resource, with businesses competing to capture and hold it.

Little did Mr. Simon know that one day, the onset of the internet, social media, texting, DMing, and the like would significantly impact this attention economy. Now the social platforms, digital marketers, and online news outlets use algorithms to personalize content and encourage engagement—"more." Nearly everything is capitalized on, fueling our desire and urges to have more. This happens not only in the marketing and social media worlds but also in the corporate world as well.

## THE ATTENTION GAME

The attention economy has become a model for the culture of many organizations. Monthly performance awards, promotions, bonuses, incentives . . . organizations are jockeying for your attention, grabbing it and enticing you to do more. They showcase their top performers, their leaders, and shine the light on them, creating a drive for you to want more and to be "one" of them.

Through this influence on corporations, the attention economy has contributed to our culture of overconsumption. The goal of influencers, marketers, and promoters is to get you to invest your attention in their product, videos, and ads, and to hold you there long enough to make a purchase. Toss in "instant gratification" via same- or next-day delivery, and it is the perfect storm for more.

## THE POTENTIAL POTHOLES OF GOING AGAINST THE NORM

Deciding to go against the norm of more can be challenging. You will be challenging *societal expectations*. Remember, society's norm of "more means better" is alive and well in our culture. It is considered the standard. When we challenge these standards and norms, their advocates may push back. They may feel threatened and react accordingly, ultimately wanting to make you wrong and themselves right. We live in a society of people wanting to look good and be right. If you are pointing out a different way that may make them look bad, their natural reaction is to flip it back on you.

Warren Buffett, a fellow Omahan, is an example of someone who chose to go against the norm of more. A billionaire, Warren lives in the same home in Omaha that he bought decades ago (I've driven by it hundreds of times). He drives a modest car and eats breakfast at McDonald's. It may seem simple, yet having some of your decisions made the day prior can be one of the best gifts you give yourself. Warren knows what breakfast looks like and thus has one less decision to make each day. Routines based on your norms matter.

In general, when you make the decision to venture against the norm, you are testing the power of your individuality! You will truly be leaning into your identities and values more than ever. To do so, you must be comfortable with and aware of what those are. There are many benefits to embracing your authenticity both professionally and personally. You may discover you are more innovative and creative than you'd thought and start living a more fulfilling life!

## THE SIMPLICITY OF ROUTINE

When we were kids, some of us had parents who laid out our clothes the night before school. No decisions to make, no stress—just get up and get dressed. That simple routine made mornings easier and set the tone for a smoother day. We had no idea what a gift this was for us.

Now, as adults, we may resist routines, regardless of whether they are complicated or simple. We may view them as a restriction of our freedom and flexibility. We may even prefer to "fly by the seat of our pants" and figure things out on the fly.

For me, rituals have proven to be the key to experiencing a better life. They are my way to experience true freedom while giving my time to the most important elements of my day and life. One of my favorite current rituals is my morning routine. It is ingrained and has become part of my formula for success. I wake up between 4 and 4:30 AM each day, with no alarm. Upon opening my eyes, I reflect on three things that I am grateful for prior to setting a foot on the ground. I turn on the coffee machine and prepare for my first cup. I move to my office, dim the lighting, and enjoy a 15-minute guided meditation. Then I turn to my journals. I have one for my general thoughts and one for my daily thought exercise, along with a special fancy pen that I only use for journaling. Then I head to the yoga studio where I participate in hot yoga and move my body. My morning routine creates the space for me to prepare for my coaching clients and position myself in a way that I can show up authentically for them. As you can imagine, there is also an evening routine.

For some of my clients, we have created a simple routine for them that has significantly improved their productivity the following day. Each night, they will plan the next day in great detail. For instance, their calendar reads "Sales Calls," and their "preplanning" actually identifies who they are going to call and their contact information. When the client shows up for work the next day, their brain is at ease, as it knows exactly what to do and has all the information necessary to execute on their day.

Other ideas of rituals you may choose to implement include the following:

- Simplify your wardrobe. Many successful leaders wear what appears to be the same outfit every day; for instance, black T-shirt, blazer, and jeans. This is the grown-up version of your parents laying out your clothing.
- Review your calendar at the end of each day and ensure you are prepared for the next day's income-producing activities (phone numbers, names, talking points, etc.).

- Wake up at the same time each day and create a powerful morning routine.
- Craft an easy-to-prepare breakfast to start the day. Set out utensils, plates, glasses, and so forth to make enjoying breakfast easier.

I'd highly encourage you to identify what activities continually get "canceled" or postponed in your schedule. Create a routine around those important activities to ensure they get executed every day. Is it finding a gym buddy to help hold you accountable, or a prayer partner to say your daily devotions in the morning, or a meal preparation service to help you with your meals? It is the little things of a routine that will make the biggest difference. Routines support our journey of the "right more."

## WHY ROUTINES WORK

Why do routines work so well? They create certainty in your life and business. Routines are a highly controllable factor in your day and allow your brain a clear direction and focus. For me, routines are decisions. Decisions are critical for guidance on what to do. When you "decide," you kill off all other options so your brain knows exactly what to do next. The power of routines and why they work is because they clear the noise and distractions that may occur without a set routine.

An important note: Not all routines are positive. Years ago, one of my coaches asked me to describe my morning to them. Not my "routine," as you will see—I was leaving out critical touch points by proudly sharing my "positive routine" elements.

I sat in silence for a moment and thought about the past week. The movie of my morning started to play in my mind, and I put myself back in my bed. "Wake up, reflect on three things I'm grateful for, get out of bed and make my way to the kitchen and turn on the coffee maker, drink some water, head to the sofa and check my phone." Then I saw it: I saw myself sitting there, phone in one hand, coffee in the other, and *boom*, right to emails and social media. I can sadly report that I was spending 15 to 45 minutes of scrolling. *Then*, the routine that I had shared with my coach started: Head to my office and begin my "positive" routine!

As I heard myself share this true routine with her, I immediately realized that I was only focused on my structured routine while tricking myself into ignoring the nonproductive actions that were truly my routine!

Do you have a routine of checking your phone immediately upon waking? Going down a social media rabbit hole? Surrendering your morning time to distractions? Are you unaware of the disempowering effects that some aspects of your routines are having?

## CHOOSING THE NORM OF LESS

When I decided to leave the company I was affiliated with during my earlier years as a coach and to lean into my individuality, so many of my peers and friends reached out to "make sure" I was doing the right thing. Many viewed leaving the "nest" as a bad decision. What I know is it stirred up some insecurities, and their reaction was more about them than me. They might have wanted to leave, too, yet they weren't ready to go against the norm. So, to make themselves feel better, they attempted to make me second-guess myself by projecting all their insecurities onto me.

This is where I had to be strong in my identities and values. Had I not been clear on those, I might have joined them in second-guessing and returned. However, I knew what I was "giving up," even as I had no idea how much I'd be receiving by creating the space for it. As big as my vision was, the reality of what I received was beyond my greatest hopes. I'm not going to say that every day was rainbows and sunshine, but the freedom to be innovative, creative, and to "change coaching up" led me to an amazing experience.

## REDEFINING SUCCESS

When you venture against the norm, you need to reflect and redefine what success is and what failure is for you. It is different outside of the lane of "more" and certainly different from the norm. Just think about how big the norm is versus stepping outside of that space. You don't hear much about anything outside the norm. In fact, you must go looking for it or create it.

I distinctly remember being at my desk about two weeks after launching reTHINK Coaching and thinking, *Wow, I am so proud of myself for making a decision that most wouldn't. For taking that leap of faith and launching a new coaching company.* I sat and looked at my roster, so proud of the names of the clients I had the privilege of working with—*and then*, it hit me: *Oh my God*, I only have eight clients. I'm used to having 40-plus clients at any given time. Coaches that have fewer than that are not good and are "dabbling" in coaching.

I started to feel my heart pound and my mind flood with disempowering thoughts. *You are failing! You have a roster that is embarrassing. You can't survive on eight clients. What were you thinking to leave all that success behind?!* You see, what I was doing was using my old company's definition of success to define my success. Their definition was focused on client count and one's ability to retain those clients.

I was beating myself up and feeling the compulsion to just find people to join my new coaching company and move them into my schedule, even if it meant filling it with clients that were not a match. When I finally gathered myself, I realized that I needed to redefine what my new success looked like. What were the parameters of success at reTHINK Coaching? The second I clarified my definition of success, I was able to breathe and think differently. I became innovative about the coaching process and how I would structure things at my company!

In creating a new model, I defined my ideal client, and then started attracting the right clients into my world. I have immense gratitude for my previous experience, as it taught me how to be a great coach and feel what success could feel like. It took a lot of work to "undo" the only definition of successful coaching that I knew and lean into my own definition! I had to create reminders and start celebrating my new wins, reinforcing my new definitions of success and creating the new norm. My "less" created so much more in my life, business, and client experience.

## JOURNEY FILLED WITH FEAR AND RESISTANCE

On the journey to deviate from the norm, you must be prepared to experience fear and resistance, both from yourself and others. When these feelings arise from within, it's a sign that you are leaving what you know behind and going in a new direction. At first, every "fail" can spark a degree of fear. You may hear yourself asking, "What if this isn't the right thing? What if I fall flat on my face and my new 'norm' doesn't work? What if the 'old' way is the only way and the right way?" When these questions come from others, you may be sensing their concern about the decisions you are making.

## THE NEED FOR CERTAINTY

I believe that one of our most important basic human needs is for certainty. When you go against the grain or the norm, you will experience uncertainty. You are venturing into new territory and lack complete clarity on how it will play out. Even though most of our need for certainty resides in the unconscious mind, it can still significantly affect our behavior. We typically do not wake up and say, "Oh, today I need to find certainty," yet our unconscious mind is constantly seeking it. Without it, our brain can feel scrambled and in a state of flux. You will most likely feel "off" and not sure why! Uncertainty can truly impact your ability to act, your reactions to things, and how you navigate your day.

## THE NORM OF FREEDOM

Another moment when I went against the norm of stability came in 2001: the moment I had to tell my parents that I was resigning from my very secure job in the hospitality industry and going into real estate. Their concern and fear bubbled up quickly. Remember, first-generation Americans often believe you should just be grateful for what you have, that you should never just walk away from something so great. My mom was the most vocal as she started questioning my decision. I know she meant no harm, yet her fear over my possible failure (and even success!) was shining through and her lack of certainty of my future was evident.

She had the hardest time accepting that I was going from job security, benefits, and a paycheck every two weeks to the unknown. Quite honestly, she would have been more accepting had I said I was joining the circus than working on commission. Had I not been strong in my convictions and spent a lot of time praying on my decision and vision, I might have freaked out! And it was not only my parents that expressed fear; many of my friends and people in my social circle could not process my decision, and a few even questioned and challenged it. I could see the doubt in their eyes.

This is a critical phase of your journey to your new norm. You have to keep others' lack of certainty from shaking your beliefs or your certainty. While my mom's concern was the hardest to wrap my brain around and understand, I knew her reaction was coming from her personal beliefs and love for me. An NLP model that I love to reference during times like this is, "Respect other people's model of the world." I do not have to agree with people; I can simply respect their model or their vision, definition, and beliefs. Once you accept those, you give their reaction a different kind of power. You respect it but keep it in its proper "lane"—theirs!

## INTERNAL RESISTANCE

The other element of resistance also reared itself during these early moments. I felt myself resisting what I knew I needed to do to be successful because it was unknown, uncomfortable, and *way* outside my comfort zone. I know this resistance was driven by my unconscious mind, yet it was a real thing to manage! My unconscious was selling me on resisting this new action; if I took it and failed, it would be a reflection on me. However, if I never acted and "failed," I really didn't fail because I didn't do anything. It was so messed up how my unconscious mind was busying itself trying to "protect" me. It was keeping me in the space of not acting, which only fueled my fear of failure.

What I now recognize my unconscious was doing was defaulting to my conditioned and habitual behaviors. I knew what to expect from those, and they created a space of certainty for me—even though this certainty was not congruent with actions that would propel my success. A study from the University of South Carolina found that 66.34% of behaviors are habitual.[20] Your mind does not see them as good or bad, just familiar, and will trade forward movement for comfort nearly every time.

As I mentioned, I also experienced resistance from the outside. Many of my friends would not use me as a Realtor®, as they didn't believe this new career was going to be long lasting, and their story of me was as a hotelier. They didn't want to support this "wild" idea, so their resistance to my new reality kept them from helping me out. Not buying into others' fears and resistance when you're breaking from your old norms is key. When someone is forming an emotion or judgment about what you are doing, it is typically a reflection of their response to the new situation. You must respect and not judge.

## CHALLENGE YOUR TRUE MOTIVATIONS

Deviating from the norm can also create interior discourse with your psychological motivations to conform or not conform. We have an overwhelming need for belonging. This quest can often conflict with your personal beliefs or values, yet the drive to belong is so strong, you tolerate those beliefs being compromised. Conforming provides a sense of social acceptance and emotional security, fostering identity within a community. This community can be your professional environment or your personal group of friends.

Another challenge you may face is the feeling of losing some of your self-identity by removing yourself from the social groups you had been connected to or the place you hold in your work organization.

## COGNITIVE DISSONANCE

Part of the struggle to stray from the norm is cognitive dissonance: when you hold two or more conflicting beliefs, values, or attitudes, especially when your behavior contradicts any of these. I think we can all relate to this. At some point in all our professional journeys, we've all had a view or idea about how something should be executed that differed from those of our colleagues or bosses. Yet, we didn't want to challenge the decision, as we didn't want to stand out, even as it directly conflicted with how we truly believed or felt about something. We may find ourselves changing our beliefs just to "fit in" with the decision made, as nonconformity would be risky and could lead to further dissonance (e.g., if no one agreed, you'd be the odd person out).

This often happened when I was in my corporate role. My creative, entrepreneurial spirit wanted to challenge many things. My brain was constantly figuring out more efficient ways to execute tasks, yet it would have taken a lot of courage to push back against the company's norm or standards. The level of frustration I would feel when I just went along with the plan, versus sharing my ideas and beliefs, was palpable. I knew I was selling myself short, yet I felt the risk of pushback was far too great for me to take that chance. I worried I wouldn't be viewed as a company person and would actually be seen as someone that was not in alignment. My fear of "not fitting in" or "being rejected" outweighed my drive to step up.

## ARE YOU READY TO RECEIVE THE GIFT OF LESS?

Are you ready to embrace intentionally choosing a different way to move about life and business? A way that goes against the norm, even those of society? A way that may feel like you are swimming upstream while everyone else is passing you by, swimming with the current? If so, you are ready to begin the clearing of more from your life and seeing your true path toward less—and success.

The journey from more to less isn't just about decluttering your physical space—though that's certainly part of it. It's about creating space in every area of your life: mental space, emotional space, and spiritual space. It's about making room for what truly matters and letting go of what doesn't support your highest purpose.

In the following chapters, we'll explore practical strategies for implementing the philosophy of less in your daily life, your relationships, your business, and your personal growth. You'll discover how to identify what truly adds value to your life and how to courageously release what doesn't. Most importantly, you'll learn how to trust the process and embrace the abundance that naturally flows when you create space for it.

The world may continue to tell you that more is better, but you will have the tools to recognize this truth: *Less is the great multiplier of more.* The question isn't whether this principle works—it's whether you're ready to trust it enough to let it transform your life.

Your journey to less starts with a single decision: to stop filling every space, every moment, every opportunity with more, and instead create room for the magic that comes when you choose intentionally, live purposefully, and trust that the universe has something better waiting for you.

Are you ready to make that choice?

## LESS OVER MORE: KEY INSIGHTS

- **Going against the norm requires courage** but leads to authentic living.
- **The "attention economy"** creates artificial urgency and FOMO.
- **Routines create certainty** and free up mental energy for what matters.
- **Resistance is natural** when changing—expect it from yourself and others.
- **Redefining success** is essential when choosing a different path.
- **66% of our behaviors** are conditioned and habitual.

# PART II

# WHEN MORE BECOMES A TRAP

## CHAPTER 4

# FROM GOAL DRIFT TO GOAL ACTIVATION

My secret bears repeating: Getting more of what we want in life isn't about chasing after more; it's about focusing on and pursuing less, which leads to the *right more.* This is true in most aspects of our lives—especially when it comes to our goals and the future we envision for ourselves. What if we could get more of what truly matters—more time, more peace, more joy, more wealth, even more business—by letting go of all the stuff that's cluttering up our lives and focusing only on the true goals that matter?

Focusing on less as a goal doesn't mean settling for less; it means making space for more of what we really need. By clearing away the unnecessary, we can fill our lives with the things that truly count. Goal-setting is an act of love—love outwardly expressed. Life is too short to live it in a loveless way.

But first we must get crystal clear on what goal-setting is really all about.

## THE WILD-ASS-GUESS ERA

What is your perspective on goal-setting? I used to view goal-setting as a task—like selecting an ambiguous target for the upcoming year. In my early days, I would refer to it as a WAG (Wild-Ass Guess) and fret over how I would create this magical forecast.

My logical mind would begin to rationalize that there were so many unknown factors outside my control. The "guess" I was making was dependent on and affected by external circumstances over which I had *no* to little control. It felt like throwing darts at a board while blindfolded, hoping something would stick.

Then one day, I was introduced to the concept of tying *emotion* to your goals and bringing them to life. I accepted that external circumstances could only impact my goals if I allowed them to do so. When you give your goals meaning like this, you become unstoppable.

## THE POWER OF EMOTION IN GOAL-SETTING

When I started to reflect on the *impact* my goals would have on me and the people in my life, suddenly the goals felt more emotional and impactful. The goals meant something. They were a clear path to providing for four important areas of my life:

1. Me
2. Family/friends
3. My team
4. My legacy

Suddenly I realized that a goal without emotion tied to it, free of any deeper meaning, meant nothing!

Every year, when I set my new goals, I immediately reflect on those four important areas of my life. This really hit home when I reflected on one of my major goals driving my business: financial freedom. *The ability to do what I want, when I want, and with who I want.*

This one overarching goal impacts *all* four areas. When I ask myself specifically what the impact will be in those four areas when my goal is achieved, goal-setting suddenly and dramatically becomes exciting. I get to feel what it will do for myself and others. To experience that emotion of making a difference is powerful.

The first time I did this, I remember feeling very uncomfortable about sharing the impact of my goals on the three factors outside of me (family/friends, team, and legacy). For the first time, I felt a level of accountability like never before. In the past, I only felt accountable to my coach; if I failed at my goals, the only person impacted by this was *me*. As soon as I brought others in, my accountability grew.

## THE ACCOUNTABILITY FACTOR

One of the keys that makes this work for me is *to share these goals* with as many people as I can, and to be willing to go to those affected by my goals and let them know if I have fallen off track.

Just the thought of having to go to my family and telling them, "Hey, you know that big, amazing trip we were going to take? I chose to not do the activities necessary to achieve that goal, and now we can't go."

Suddenly, the goal is not just a number—it has a face and experience attached to it. It has emotion and feels very alive. This brings me closer to my goals and helps me do the activities that I may not naturally want to do. It can be the driver that helps me make that one additional sales call, go to that networking event that I'd rather skip, or not play on social media during my sales time.

I promise you, there is nothing more gratifying than seeing your goals and their direct impact on others.

## THE GOAL-GRAVEYARD PHENOMENON

You may be able to relate to this pattern: We write out our goals, we get excited about what they can do for us, and in that moment, we feel energized. Then comes time to act. Usually by this time, we have stashed away our plans and goals in a folder and haven't looked at them for a long time.

We go back to "doing," but not necessarily doing the needed actions, because we are detached from our goals. Then at the end of the quarter (or worse, on October 1), we think about our goals and where we are in relation to them. We typically have a gap between "actual" and "goal." This gap feels like a canyon at times, yet we decide to close it, ultimately creating an extremely stressful environment for ourselves. We may end up resenting the very goals we once felt excited about.

I've seen this happen all too often with business owners, and it typically happens near the end of the third quarter of the year, creating a very unpleasant final quarter and disrupting their happiness.

I was able to break this cycle by attaching impact and emotions to the goals. I began looking forward to visiting my goals daily, weekly, monthly, and quarterly. They were not long "one-day goals," they were my future and the future of those who would benefit from the payoff. By no means was this easy. What made it work was making the connection genuine and meaningful. When I connected to the impact, it landed with me in a way that motivated me to take action and move toward the goals.

## EVOLUTION VERSUS RECYCLING: WHY GOALS MUST GROW

How many times have you found yourself ending the year short of your goal and then using that same goal you didn't achieve for the next year? Maybe you increased it minimally just to feel good and trick yourself into thinking you're moving forward. Or you came up with amazing stories as to why the upcoming year will be different.

I think we all have had a period in our business and lives where we have experienced the same month over and over, the same year over and over. We didn't understand why, yet it was happening! Our goals truly didn't evolve—they were recycled. This can be frustrating if you're living in the space of "more," as your desires to accumulate more can be intoxicating yet frustrating when not met.

However, as you gain experience and have a clearer understanding of the world, the impact you desire to make becomes more important to you, and your goals evolve. The clearer you are about what is possible, the more you begin to see things through a different lens.

Let's look at internal and external factors that affect how your goals evolve.

### Internal Factors

- **Self-Discovery and Personal Growth:** As you learn about your strengths, weaknesses, and interests, you may reset your goals to be more congruent with these changes. These discoveries can influence what you believe to be important, affecting your internal drivers and ultimately your goals.
- **Learning and Experience:** We are not static—we are constantly learning and experiencing new things. These experiences and learnings can profoundly affect the goals you set for

yourself and your business. The more you know, the more you can do.

- **Personal Growth:** As your life and your business evolve, you may look at your goals through a completely different lens and feel a shift. Perhaps you want more time with your family and friends, or you want to start a family, or the values of the business you're affiliated with change. This growth is real and may cause you to reassess things.

**External Factors**

- **Changes in Market Conditions:** As market conditions evolve, priorities often shift. Goals that once seemed essential may lose relevance, requiring reevaluation.
- **Technology:** Your goals may no longer be relevant because technology has undergone substantial changes and made them obsolete. (Think Blockbuster, fax machines, pagers, etc.)
- **Shifts in Social and Cultural Conditions:** What was once acceptable or desired may no longer be relevant in our new world. As society evolves, some of our goals may become outdated.
- **Economic Changes:** Changes to our world economy also can affect your goals. Recessions, depressions, inflation, stagflation, and booming economies can all influence your potential—if you allow them to.

## CLARITY IS POWER: HOW I WAS TRAPPED BY OTHERS' DREAMS

Your goals should reflect the highest objective in your life. Yet, at some point, we take on someone else's idea of what our goals can be or should be.

This may have started at a young age. Think about when we meet with our guidance counselors in high school. I remember hearing about these meetings from my friends who'd already had theirs. I was thinking, *Wow, how awesome to figure out what I get to do next*, and felt excited at the prospect.

My time came to meet, and I think I was just as excited about being able to leave in the middle of one of my boring classes as I was to go talk about my future! Walking toward the counselor's office, I had great hopes of how the conversation would go.

As I sat down, I remember the counselor asking me what I wanted to do next. "Oh, I am so excited to be done with school. I can't wait to be able to work and make my own money to be able to live on my own and do what I want."

I remember the counselor looking at me with a very perplexed look on their face. They said, "No, what do you want to do for your profession? You can't just not go to school and make money."

I sat there and felt all the excitement and vision I had for my future drain from my body. I felt lost and a bit foolish for even sharing my vision. It was as if someone snapped their fingers in my face, wiped away my goals, and pushed their own options onto me—*all* of which required formal education and a path that I had never considered taking. I just wanted the meeting to be over, so I agreed on being a "businessman" and getting a general degree in business. I left feeling very deflated.

Between my parents' push for university and the counselor's guidance, I took on their goals. Go to university, get a bachelor's degree, and get a job. Their goals became mine, and I started living it. While I'm grateful for the push and having a degree, the reality is my goal never would have included university education. I hated school and most things about it. Outside of the social aspect, school and classes and syllabi were not my thing, ever. It felt very restricting to me, and I dreaded most everything about it.

Sadly, living someone else's goal of higher education was honestly a struggle for me. My parents were *huge* higher education people, and it was a nonnegotiable with them. They scrimped and saved for each of us to go to college and graduate with no debt. They expected their goal to be my goal. I'd never "failed" courses before, yet in college I actually got an F and numerous D's. How do you get an F in astronomy? Well, it is possible. Ultimately, I had zero positive emotion attached to the goal of a college degree. It didn't matter to me, and I truly resented that era of my life.

## THE CORPORATE GOAL TRAP

As I embarked on my professional career in the hotel industry, I scratched the surface of living my true life and saw the opportunity to take control of my goals. Yet my goals were also dictated by a path that leadership saw as the route to get to the next level. The organizational chart imposed many steps for getting to desired positions, which required me to accept someone else's "goals" and pathway.

I know I leaned into other goals early in my career with Marriott and honestly was unclear about my direction with the company. I didn't know the many paths I could take within the organization, and because I wasn't committed to any real goals, I started to absorb other people's goals. I was fortunate that I met two incredible leaders, Dale and Klayton, early on in my career, who loaned me a set of goals to follow. In fact, they were the ones who encouraged me to apply for certain positions, which ultimately led to my amazing path forward with Marriott. I was so fortunate that they both came from a place of high integrity and truly had my best interests in mind. If their goals for me had been to help them support their own goals and only contribute to their future success, I could have ended up in a very different situation! My lack of clarity on my big goals made me very vulnerable.

## WHAT CLARITY PROVIDES

With all the external "more" noise, how can you identify your highest objective in life through the goals you choose for yourself, through clarity? Clarity is the first step in creating a clear map for your brain to follow and to achieve your true goals. Our goals should provide many things for you:

- **Purpose and Direction:** Goals act as a roadmap and provide clarity for your life, providing a clear sense of purpose. They can direct your efforts, helping you with decisions and strategies. When we don't have clear objectives, we are susceptible to taking on others' goals and feeling somewhat "lost" or without direction.
- **Personal Growth:** When you have meaningful goals, you will discover that you need to learn new skills, work on your disciplines, and expand what you can do. This process builds your confidence and resilience toward your next set of goals. With each win and achievement, you further realize your true potential and tackle challenges more effectively. You will also navigate failure differently when you are attached to your goals versus someone else's; failing at someone else's goals will have a less significant impact.
- **Motivation Booster:** Goals certainly assist with your motivation! Clarity on where you're headed is exciting, and you can lean into this excitement as you begin your journey. The little wins along the way fuel your motivation and keep you moving forward even when things get tough.

- **Decision-Making:** Decisions become so much easier when you know your goals. Saying yes to the right things happens naturally, and more importantly, saying *no* to the things that will take you off course becomes easier.
- **Personal Satisfaction:** There is a euphoria that fills you when you have meaningful goals that help you achieve your highest objectives in life and business. They naturally improve your sense of worth and self-esteem.
- **A Richer, Fulfilling Life:** When your highest objectives in life are being met and align with your true values, they add meaning to your life. The goals provide you with a framework through which you can make a deep impact in your world.
- **Growth Mindset:** On your journey to your goals, you will face challenges and failures. Yet the goals are so compelling that you will take the failures as lessons and figure out your way forward. This may involve hiring a coach, taking a course, or joining a group with mentorship, all of which keep you in a state of forward momentum and embracing the learning. Sometimes you win, and sometimes you *learn*!
- **Long-Term Vision:** Goals that fulfill your highest objectives in life and business help you see your future in a new way. You can think bigger and see endless opportunities. You start to experience the emotion of your future as if it has already happened. Your brain sees the long-term vision as a possibility and begins working toward that future with direction and passion.

What I love about the brain is that when you see or create your long-term vision, you are literally creating your future. We don't spend enough time in this place. We typically spend time in our past (what worked, what didn't work, what should have or could have) or our present. We need to become more intentional about spending time in our future—living into it as if it has already happened, allowing ourselves to experience the emotions and impact of the goals being accomplished. Your brain will adapt and start to create the "how" that will bring this future to life.

## BRACE FOR IMPACT: THE RIPPLE EFFECT OF YOUR GOALS

Just as goals without meaning are meaningless, if you are unaware of the *impact of your goals*, the goals will fall short. Every goal you have should ripple through your life, business, and the people who are part of both.

The first time you sort through your traditional "more" goals, the greater your shock may be when you uncover their impact. You may believe the goal—achieving a title, getting a promotion, or taking a vacation—might only affect you, versus the world and those you love. Yet, when you incorporate into your goal an awareness of the difference you will make in the external world (friends, family, peers, strangers, legacy), you will become crystal clear on the impact your goal can have and the responsibility that comes with that.

Suddenly it's not about a new title on a business card or on LinkedIn. Instead, it may be about becoming a leader who lifts those around you—who provides the space for others to excel and achieve their goals that make a difference in their own external worlds.

It took me a moment to realize that much of my success was directly tied to those I surrounded myself with—my employees, doing the work necessary to reach our goals. One of my favorite quotes is from Roy T. Bennett, in his book *The Light in the Heart*: "Always remember people who have helped you along the way, and don't forget to lift someone up."

To me, this means taking into consideration the impact of your goals on not only yourself, but your family and friends, your team, and your legacy. Suddenly, your strategies and actions reach far beyond just you. They have greater meaning.

## THE CALIENDO LEGACY

One of my early ventures into setting goals with an impact far outside of me—one that did not involve me "getting more"—was the year I established a scholarship in my parents' name.

As the only boy in our immediate family, me not having kids meant the Caliendo name would not carry forward. While my parents didn't say much about it, the few times it came up in conversation, I could see how important it was to them. I sat with this thought for years, struggling to figure out a way to honor the Caliendo name, my parents' legacy, and help it continue.

It came to me: I would establish a Caliendo Scholarship at the university my dad graduated from, and the nursing school my mom attended (attached to the same university). Education was extremely important to my parents. This goal checked off several items on my "impact" list—honoring my parents' legacy, fulfilling something meaningful for myself, and providing financial assistance to deserving students.

For me, it was a true driver. Not only was my ability to fund this scholarship aiding one of my goals, it was also improving the recipient's experience. I had the scholarship set up to be given to a freshman and to fund their education through graduation. This goal was not a one and done; it was ongoing. It had meaning and impact and therefore was a true driver for me.

This is what happens when we move from "more" goals with no impact to powerful goals that influence others—the impact becomes exponentially greater while the complexity becomes beautifully simpler.

## AGENCY AND THE POWER OF CHOICE

Discovering that you have the power and ability to make your own choices and decisions—to act independently, to be in control of your own actions and life, and to set your own goals—is one of the greatest gifts you can receive. Give yourself permission to truly set goals that you desire and to show yourself grace when they drift and change.

### *Why Goals Drift*

Why do goals drift and change? Often, it's because of value drift. You no longer see the value in the goals you set. You either have an awakening that the goals are no longer providing the value you deserve or desire, or you take a stand for yourself and set your own goals versus adopting others'.

Another gift of agency is realizing that our "less" goals may seem much simpler than our "more" goals, yet they create greater results and bigger impact. Adapting to simpler goals can take a moment. If you have lived in the space of "more" and have had grandiose goals, your simpler "less" goals may initially seem insignificant. In addition, when you take the goal spotlight off yourself, you will clear space to set goals with a further reach!

### *The Congruency Factor*

The important element to keep in mind about simpler or "less" goals is that they provide the brain with a sense of peace and congruency. It may be the first time you have felt congruent with the goals you have set because they match your internal vibration—the vibration that you may have been ignoring up to this point, the one that has been quietly "screaming" in the background. Now you are truly hearing it and allowing it to have a voice.

The power of agency is an amazing gift. When you claim it, you step into the truth that less truly can create more—not just in your possessions or commitments, but in the very goals that shape your life's direction.

## *Balance: It's Not About the Money*

Remember, goals that don't arise from your agency are meaningless. Goals that are targeted toward making more money for the sake of more can be the least fulfilling when you achieve them. If your goal is based on the "more money model," it may be focused on very materialistic things and have a short "satisfaction" shelf life.

On my journey to less, I learned an extremely valuable lesson from one of my dear mentors. She shared, "It's not about the money, but what the money can do." That was a moment of clarity; while money is important, its main purpose is to "do good" in the world.

When we choose less in our goal-setting—fewer goals with deeper meaning, simpler objectives with greater impact—we create space for what truly matters. We stop chasing the next promotion, the next purchase, the next validation, and we start building the life we actually want to live. We create the space for more impactful opportunities than those we may have been chasing or forcing.

This is goal activation at its finest: not the frantic pursuit of more, but the intentional cultivation of what matters most. And in that space of less, we discover we have room for so much more than we ever imagined possible.

## LESS OVER MORE: KEY INSIGHTS

- **Goals without emotion are meaningless,** so you must attach deep personal impact to every goal by considering how it affects you, your family, your team, and your legacy.
- **Stop recycling and start evolving,** because goals should grow and change as you do. Repeating the same objectives year after year signals stagnation, not progress.
- **Claiming your agency** requires breaking free from goals imposed by others (parents, employers, society), and choosing objectives that align with your authentic values.
- **Impact over achievement** means the most meaningful goals create ripple effects beyond yourself. Ask, "What difference will this make?" not just, "What will I get?"
- **Less complexity, more results** is a strategy that works because simpler goals with deeper meaning consistently outperform grandiose objectives.

CHAPTER 5

# THE MAGIC OF RIGHTSIZING VERSUS WRONGSIZING

The magic of a "less" mindset is a gift—and it's one I want to share with you. This gift needs some assembling, and in this chapter, I am going to provide you with the how-to steps to experience this gift and all the amazing benefits that come with it.

Get ready, because this first step is one of the most powerful choices you can make toward a life that is "rightsized." I call this step "magic" because when I learned about it, it was as if someone had pulled the curtain back and showed me the greatest magic trick ever.

A note of caution: This shift may create some friction in your current thought patterns and the mindset you hold around success or a big life. Know that this is okay. The greatest times of growth happen when we are uncomfortable. Let's get comfortable with being uncomfortable and trust the process. And let's start that process by understanding the difference between rightsizing and wrongsizing.

## RIGHTSIZING VERSUS WRONGSIZING: THE FOUNDATION

What is rightsizing versus wrongsizing? Rightsizing is arranging your life in a manner that creates balance. You are enjoying the journey to success in all areas of your life. It's about ridding yourself of things that are no longer serving you and creating space in your world for the amazing to show up.

Wrongsizing is what so many of us have done on our journey of evolution—how we built our lives and filled them with things, ideas, beliefs, and philosophies of what we accepted as the path to success. There is no judgment, and you aren't "wrong." You simply allowed the construct of your life to unfold in a way that may no longer be useful or was based on old thoughts and an outdated mindset.

Take a moment right now to think of your definition of "more" and "less." What do these words mean to you? What story or ideas do you have around them? How have they impacted your life and beliefs in the past? There's no right or wrong answer—just your truth.

In the beginning, when I thought of more and less in the traditional sense, I viewed more as positive and empowering. The more you had, the more evidence there was of your success. Likewise, less symbolized less success. Having less was a sign of weakness. Both perceptions had a tremendous impact on my mindset and beliefs of how life and business works. However, after reframing and redefining, I now understand that more is not always the path to empowerment and living a big life.

## UNDERSTANDING MINDSET: YOUR MENTAL SUNGLASSES

Let's get on the same page about mindset. One of the questions I often get as a coach is, does mindset cause thoughts, or do thoughts cause your mindset? My answer is: Yes. I believe they are interdependent.

Think of your mindset as a pair of sunglasses—a filter you look through to see the world. Everything you see when wearing them is changed and affected by the color of the lens, influencing in turn how and what you see, feel, and experience.

Likewise, think of your thoughts like choosing a pair of sunglasses. The lenses you pick change how you see the world around you. Your mindset shapes those thoughts, and those thoughts shape your mindset.

## DEFINITIONS THAT MATTER

Mindset is often defined as:

- The established set of attitudes you hold
- A collection of beliefs and thoughts
- A mental attitude, inclination, tendency, or habit

My definition of mindset:

- Your beliefs and your interpretation of stories you have created and/or adopted that affect your decisions, outcomes, and overall self

Thoughts are often defined as:

- Specific mental content
- Ideas, opinions, and memories
- May include worries
- Fleeting and can change rapidly
- Don't require effort or even conscious control

My definition of thoughts:

- Stories your brain creates to process and understand what is happening. Something you give meaning to based on past experiences or external influences.
- A reaction to a situation or external circumstance that you are experiencing, based on your existing emotional state or mindset.

## THE EXTERNAL HIJACKING OF YOUR MIND

I believe our mindset is easily influenced by external sources. Before I became aware that I could "control" my mindset and thoughts, they were often influenced by others. You wake up in one state of mind—perhaps happy, carefree, excited about the day. Then, you turn on the news and hear about an event in the global economy or local news that dulls or darkens your mood. Suddenly, your mindset has shifted to concerned and doubtful. You took on other people's stories or opinions, and it shifted your mindset.

Mindset is easily influenced and can pull you around from highs and lows multiple times a day, an hour, or even by the minute.

## THE INFORMATION OVERLOAD CRISIS

We live in a time when we are bombarded by information. Much of the information we consume is filtered through someone else's lens—corporations, producers, networks with agendas. Depending on which network you prefer, the same news story can be portrayed in a different light by each channel. One may spin this story to have a positive effect and the other, a negative one. The lens they report it through determines how you end up feeling.

You must become diligent about protecting your space and your awareness if you truly want to steer your thoughts and mindset.

## MY PERSONAL INFORMATION DETOX: THE NUMBERS DON'T LIE

Early in 2020, during the onset of the coronavirus pandemic, we were watching the news and staying up to date. I realized that prior to the "update," the music that led into the story was rather ominous. I likened it to the music you hear while watching a horror movie when you know something bad is about to happen. There I was, sitting and waiting to learn what was going on, then—enter the "horror" music. At this moment, I realized the network news was casting an experience on its listeners. For me, the experience made my thoughts and mindset scared and anxious. At that moment, I made the decision to no longer watch the news—to protect my mindset and thoughts from the external influence of others.

## MY SHOCKING TIME AUDIT

I discovered during this time that, on average, Americans consume news for approximately three hours per day . . . and I was very much like the average American. I had been starting my day by turning on a national morning news show. Hearing the program's opening theme start was a comforting ritual—or so I'd thought.

When I sat with this statistic, I immediately thought of the compound effect. Three hours per day times 350 days of the year (with some vacation time) equaled 1,050 hours of my life given to absorbing the news—someone else's thoughts and mindset. The equivalent of 43 days. *Yikes!* I was giving up 1½ months of my year to news?

I made the decision, on my path to less, to consume my news through a service that strictly provides the facts and allows me to formulate my own thoughts or do further research for clarity. I allowed myself 30 minutes per day to take in different sources of news, giving myself back the equivalent of 36 days, and ultimately controlling the information affecting my mindset and thoughts.

## MY SOCIAL MEDIA REVELATION

Next on my quest toward less was my awareness of social media and consuming information from it. Though I had disconnected from the news, my social media feeds were now full of news stories. Along with the news came all the people I was following who gave their interpretation of events, full of personal opinions and predictions, most based on assumptions versus fact. And I wasn't alone; I discovered that, on average, we spend about 2 hours and 21 minutes per day browsing social media.[21] Not all of that time is taking in news, but we are still absorbing information, along with others' thoughts and interpretations. Running the numbers on this was another eye opener. Across the same 350-day year, this equated to 845 hours on social media, or just over 35 whole days.

I therefore set boundaries around social media too. While I have a place for it in my business, I could certainly protect my time better. I committed to no more than 30 minutes per day on social media, which gave me back the equivalent of almost 28 days.

The bottom line: Given that time is one of our most valuable assets, reclaiming 64 days (36 days from the news and 28 days from social media) and experiencing less was a complete game changer for me. I not only protected my mindset and thoughts, I also created space for what is truly important in my life: family, friends, creative time, and so much more. Ultimately, I created a barrier against the data I absorb from social media and the impact it has on my mindset and thoughts.

## YOUR INFORMATION DETOX CHALLENGE

Thirty-Day Information Detox Exercise:

1. Track your current news and social media consumption for one week.
2. Calculate your yearly hours (daily minutes × 350 days, or 365 calendar days minus your days off from work).
3. Set new boundaries: 30 minutes of news, 30 minutes of social media maximum.
4. Use the reclaimed time for activities that align with your "less over more" goals.
5. Notice the shift in your mindset and energy levels.

Be prepared for pushback. People may call you irresponsible or uninformed. To be honest, most people prefer to remain oblivious to how much time they lose to social media and the news, as both have become engrained in their day-to-day lives.

# THE GAME-CHANGING THOUGHT FLOW MODEL

Your thoughts often have a greater impact on your results than your actions alone. In my coaching practice, we use our Thought Flow Model, which demonstrates that all results in life and business are ultimately driven by our thoughts. This model is rooted in Dr. Aaron Beck's ABC Model, first introduced in the 1950s.

The ABC Model suggests that external events (A) do not directly cause emotions (C); rather, it is our beliefs (B)—especially irrational beliefs—that shape our emotional responses. In essence, thoughts are beliefs, and they can either empower or disempower us.

The model shows how thoughts flow through to results. You can also work the model from bottom up—if you are not pleased with your results, reflect on your actions, feelings, and thoughts that drove those. You do not have to wait for the result to tap into this model. If you are experiencing a negative feeling, emotion, or energy, stop and explore what thought is creating that.

The Thought Flow Model that we use is as follows:

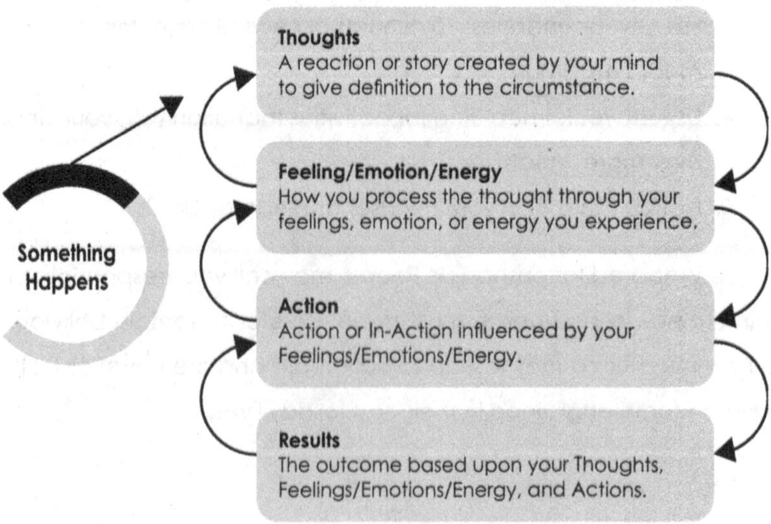

### *The Thought Flow Model in Action*

Example: Economic Uncertainty

**Something Happens:** External economic shifts cause consumer confidence to drop.

**Thought:** "I'm not going to be able to navigate this change, and my business is going to drop significantly or completely. No one will spend money right now."

**Feeling/Energy/Emotion:** "I'm feeling stressed, lack energy to even show up, and I'm feeling down."

**Actions:** Freeze up and do nothing *or* take action—even with severe doubt—and receive more "no's" than "yeses."

**Results:** Business is significantly down, and sales are nearly nonexistent.

*The Alternative Thought:* "Economic shifts create opportunities for those who serve people's real needs. I can focus on providing more value with less complexity."

*New Results:* Focused action, better client relationships, sustainable business growth.

## YOUR THOUGHT FLOW EXERCISE

Take a moment to apply this model:

1. Identify a current challenge or negative result you're experiencing.
2. Work from results to thoughts (reverse): What actions led to this result?
3. What feelings/energy drove those actions?

4. What specific thought created those feelings?
5. Now create an alternative, empowering thought.
6. Run the new thought through the model and see the different outcome.

## THE CONCEPT OF LESS: REDEFINING SUCCESS

How you define less depends on two things: your thoughts and your mindset. Having lived in the more space for a long time and for multiple careers, I didn't immediately embrace the concept of less. My thoughts were running wild with catastrophic thinking: "If I give up more and leave this structure, what if this less thing doesn't work? Can I recover, or will I be starting over?"

I knew in my heart it was time to embrace the philosophy of less, yet up until this point, my entire life and career was based on more. In a way, it felt like I was giving up all that I worked for—the position in life and business that many would be happy to have—and here I was, thinking of "less." I didn't know immediately that "less" was going to be my approach. I just knew that I was out of sync with myself and something was off.

## THE QUIET REVELATION

It was in the quiet moments of my day and life when it really hit me. My biggest struggle with the quiet came at night, when I would lay my head on the pillow and finally allow myself to think about making a change. I had *a lot* of questions for myself: "Are you just tired? Do you need a vacation? Do you need to hire a personal assistant? Do you need someone who can exert more leverage to take some of your workload? Are you being selfish? Are you being ungrateful for what you have? Are you just burned out?"

I worked through this with my coach and realized that it was time for me to "wring out the sponge."

What does less mean to you? When you think of less, what story or definition are you drawing from to create your understanding? Take a moment and gain clarity for yourself. There is no right or wrong, just your meaning. Knowing this can be key in unlocking your mindset and moving toward the magic of rightsizing.

## DISTINGUISHING LESS FROM SCARCITY

Less is *not* about scarcity. Scarcity is truly not having enough and typically is not a choice that people make. There was a time early on in my real estate career that I experienced true scarcity. My liquid funds were exhausted, and I had to make a choice between paying my car note and my rent. That is scarcity.

Less is also *not* a scarcity move. It is an intentional move to release all that is no longer moving you forward so you can create space for what truly empowers you in life and business. You may be wondering, "Giving up what doesn't empower me or move me forward to make room for other things doesn't sound like more." Correct: It is not more; it is more of the right thing(s).

Take this inventory exercise:

- What is your "more" right now?
- What are you filling the space with?
- What are your thoughts on your situation of more?

You might be feeling all sorts of emotions—pride, shame, frustration, excitement, happiness—or even no emotion at all. There is no right or wrong, yet as we move toward the magic of less, your more will take on a different meaning.

## HOW 20% GETS YOU MORE: THE PARETO PRINCIPLE APPLIED

A great lesson about how less can work for you lies in the Pareto Principle. This principle states that 20% of your activities will account for 80% of your results. This concept has been around for decades, and while not proven mathematically to be exact, there is enough evidence for its truth. If 20% of your efforts lead to 80% of your results, does this mean 80% of your activities are not as impactful?

Being busy or playing in the 80% is not the same as being productive. We have all witnessed or been the person who has had a *busy* day . . . yet, at the end of the day, spent a lot of time doing things, never getting the results we truly desire.

## THE ENTREPRENEUR'S TRAP

It is not uncommon for entrepreneurs and small business owners to feel that they need to work excessive hours to produce profits and avoid working for someone else. There is a saying about entrepreneurs: "We are the only people that will work 80 hours a week to avoid working for someone else for 40 hours per week."

How do you avoid this?

1. Write down the activities you complete to achieve your goals.
2. Narrow down the activities to the top 20% that net you the biggest return on investment of your time and results.
3. Focus solely on those activities—you will get 80% of your results or goals.
4. Make your 20% activities *nonnegotiable.*

## CLIENT SUCCESS STORY: REAL TRANSFORMATION

Watching this principle come to life is truly rewarding. During the course of my coaching career, the 80/20 rule, mindset, and thought work have helped many of my clients do less and get more. It truly is a fascinating process to watch unfold.

One of my clients, who trusted the process of focusing on less, experienced true success. It was a season in real estate when many agents were experiencing a challenging year. We shifted our mindset and truly strategized about what critical activities always brought business. We crafted a plan, created the path forward, and trusted that this focus on fewer of the right activities would bring us the greatest results.

This took discipline and daily thought work. She had to work on her mindset and thoughts to keep the faith and belief that her success was possible—regardless of external market conditions. As a result, she had an amazing year and, compared to many of her peers, outperformed the market.

Yet this was much more than about selling more homes. This clearing of "do more" allowed her to live her life at a higher level. She was able to enjoy time with her daughter and the life she is building. Having just completed a massive renovation on her home, she engaged this freedom to have more space for amazing memories and experiences. None of the external noise mattered any longer, and neither did the "shiny object syndrome" to do other things. She hunkered down, focused on her proven strategies, and crushed it!

Thought work is a strategy that we must treat like business strategies. You can't just say, "I'm going to change my thoughts" and they magically change. You must do the work and have daily activities that help you shift and change your thoughts and mindset. The Thought Flow Model is one of the strategies that I highly recommend if you wish to change your mindset and create a new result and outcome. This is what we call Thought Strategy work.

## THE WIN-THE-DAY SCORECARD

How can you position yourself to win? One of the strategies I have implemented for myself and my clients is to create a "Win-the-Day Scorecard." On this scorecard, I have my 20% identified and am clear that these actions are nonnegotiable. I use this scorecard to ensure I am staying on track and focused on the 20% versus the noise of the 80%.

At first, I would grab my scorecard before going to lunch. I'd assess where I was, and if I was falling short or failing, I could course-correct by the end of the day. As I improved and my 20% became my habit, I shifted to scoring myself at the end of the day. Both processes allowed me to catch things in the now and not allow the accumulation of time off task to keep me from my goal.

The other power in the Win-the-Day Scorecard is how it helped manage my saying yes or no to things. If I was asked to do something or tempted to try something new, I could simply look at my scorecard, and if the ask was in alignment with my 20%, I could say yes. If it wasn't, the "no" came much easier.

Create your Win-the-Day Scorecard:

1. Identify your 20% activities (3–5 maximum).
2. Make them measurable and specific.
3. Score yourself daily (1–10 scale).
4. Use it as a filter for new opportunities.
5. Celebrate consistency over perfection.

## MINDSET AND THOUGHT CHANGE: THE BYRON KATIE METHOD

How do we change our mindset, our thoughts, or the thoughts that create our mindset? One of my favorite tools for changing disempowering thoughts or mindset comes from the talented Byron Katie. She offers four simple questions that can turn things around quickly and get you grounded in empowering thoughts and mindset beliefs.[22]

The Four Questions to ask about the disempowering thought you are having:

1. Is it true?
2. Can you absolutely know it is true?
3. How do you react? What happens when you believe that thought?
4. Who would you be without the thought?

Then, turn this thought around!

**The reTHINK Four Question Model**

1. Is the thought true or just familiar? (Remember, we have up to around 60,000 thoughts per day; 80% are negative and 95% are repetitive or familiar.[23])
2. What is the loop you are running? (The loop refers to 95% of our thoughts being repetitive.)
3. Thank and dismiss the loop, as it is no longer needed.
4. What is the new thought?

## EXAMPLE: "LESS WILL MAKE ME LESS SUCCESSFUL"

Let's run through an example so you can see how this works. Take the disempowering thought of "Less will make me less successful," which is creating a mindset of doubt and fear.

1. *Is it true?* In the moment, based upon the situation and your mindset, you absolutely may think that this thought is true! That's okay, as this is the reality of what your thoughts and mindset are experiencing.
    - *Your answer might be: "HECK YES, THIS IS TRUE."*
2. *Can you absolutely know it is true?* I think of this as "Is it 100% true?" Is it absolutely true every time? What I like about this question is that rarely anything is 100% true *all* the time. This simple yet powerful question does an amazing job of opening the door to the possibility of a different outcome. You just need a glimmer of hope that there can be another way.
    - *Your answer might be: "I do know people that do a lot less than I do and are successful, so it is possible that this thought of being less successful is not true."*
3. *How do you react? What happens when you believe that thought?* What Katie is asking here is: When you believe the thought is true, how do you show up? What is the impact on you and your experience? This gets you to pause to see how you are currently showing up by believing this disempowering thought or living into the negative mindset.
    - *Your answer might be: "I show up afraid that I will be less successful and judged by others. That I'm risking it all, and by taking less, I'm agreeing to reducing my place in the world."*

4. *Who would you be without the thought?* Wow! This is the game changer. This is where you get to see what your options are and decide how you want to show up. You release the "story" you are holding around the thought, then get to redefine it. *This* is *powerful*, as it can become your truth!
   - *Your answer might be: "I get to experience less and the joy that will bring to my life. This can allow different things to come to me that I have been blocking for years, ultimately allowing me to live my truer life and enjoy my intended goals and business."*

The turnaround: Rewrite the thought and state it for yourself. *"Less will not make me less successful and will actually create the space for different and potentially more success or joy in my life."*

Your turn: What is one thought you repeatedly have that is not serving you? Take a moment and think about it. Once you come up with the disempowering thought you have over and over or the one you want to change, run it through the Four Questions. Feel the energy shift and the possibility of a different way present itself to you.

The reTHINK Four Questions are based on the fact that we have over 60,000 thoughts per day with 80% of those being negative and 95% being repetitive.

Let's take that same example so you can see how this works. Consider how the disempowering thought of "Less will make me less successful" is creating a mindset of doubt and fear.

- Is the thought true or just familiar?
  — *It is not true, and it is one of my potential 48,000 (negative thoughts) that I am experiencing on replay. So, it is truly just familiar.*

- What is the loop I'm running?
  — *This is my "fear" loop. The one that keeps me from making changes based upon my thoughts.*
- Thank and dismiss the loop.
  — *Thank you, "fear" loop. The thought isn't true, and you do not need to protect me from making changes based on fear of failure.*
- What is the new thought?
  — *"I get to experience less and the joy that will bring to my life. This can allow different things to come to me that I have been blocking for years, ultimately allowing me to live my truer life and enjoy my intended goals and business."*
  — *Less is a great path toward the right more.*

## THE SPILLOVER EFFECT: RIGHTSIZING EVERYTHING

The gift of rightsizing is possible in all aspects of our lives: home life, relationships, business, finances, and so forth. I hold the belief that "how you do one thing is how you do everything," and the simplicity of rightsizing in one area will spill over to the others.

The moment I started rightsizing my home life, everything was exponentially better in all areas of my life. I had more time for my family; I was experiencing more joy. I found it easier to say no to things that were not honoring my "less" movement or my 20%. You see, in my home life, I also had a 20% that brought me 80% of my joy. Quality time with my family and friends increased, as did my joy factor.

**Reflection Questions**

- What is your 20% for your home life? Is it a date night with your spouse? Happy hour with your friends? Genuine conversation with your spouse or friends with no interruptions?

- What is your 20% for your relationships, business, finances, and freedoms?

I want you to feel the relief of letting go of the 80% noise and distractions and the peace the 20% can and will bring your way.

## THE TRANSFORMATION MINDSET

Our mindset and thoughts shape every outcome in our lives and business. Consider it from the perspective of pursuing a "more life." I experienced this firsthand and only realized the toll it was taking on me when I found myself exhausted and frustrated with my "dream life," which felt more like a nightmare. The hectic pace I maintained in my quest for more was draining and detrimental to my overall well-being.

Yet because my mindset and thoughts were founded in the "more" mentality, I never questioned this path until I experienced being "sick and tired of being sick and tired." My thoughts finally changed, and my mindset followed. You may find yourself in this same situation. You may be so accustomed to your routines that you ignore the signs indicating there might be a different way. This cycle becomes your normal, preventing you from questioning either the process or the results you are experiencing.

As we continue to solidify a life-of-less mindset and the magic of rightsizing, allow yourself to be open to the process. Avoid getting stuck in the how, as we will continue to uncover that as we move forward together. Trust that the how will show up on a "need-to-know basis" and will become clear to you as you reset your mindset and experience the impact of rightsizing.

You now have the right mindset—that is, you have rightsized your mindset for less. And this will yield more dividends than you can possibly imagine. In the next chapter, we'll take this foundation and apply it to the practical areas of your life, starting with your personal environment and energy. The magic is just beginning.

## LESS OVER MORE: KEY INSIGHTS

- **Your mindset is your mental sunglasses,** and they filter everything you see and experience, so choose your lens intentionally.
- **External forces hijack your thinking,** so protect your mental space by limiting news consumption and curating your information diet.
- **The Thought Flow Model** drives all results as your thoughts create feelings, which drive actions, which produce results.
- **The 80/20 principle is life changing** as you focus on the 20% of activities that produce 80% of your results and eliminate the rest.
- **Rightsizing creates spillover effects:** When you rightsize one area of life, the positive effects naturally flow into all other areas.

# PART III

# LIVING MORE OF LESS

CHAPTER 6

# ONE PERCENT OFF COURSE

What gives less its power? I'll give you a hint: the absence of more. But even more than that, less gets its oomph from two key words: focus and leverage.

The *more* focus you place on fewer things, the *less* you spread yourself across time, priorities, money, or relationships—the *more* leverage you create. It might sound backward, but it's true. Mind you, less is not deprivation; it is a *deliberate* choice for and about what matters. Subtracting noise and removing choices allows you to amplify clarity, creativity, and calm. Less is about leverage, not about loss.

This deliberate choice or decision for less can change everything in your life and business. You may feel the pull toward this decision as you begin to feel out of alignment and no longer congruent with any old definition of success. And the decision will bring with it questions.

How do you remove the excess and focus on the less, the fewer, the highest-quality and best things for you? The answer is that getting to less takes patience. It is a sorting process to move from the many to the few. And it's truly life changing in its power.

But before I show you how to harness this power, let me tell you about the day I discovered I was completely off course—and didn't even know it.

## THE FLIGHT PLAN I NEVER INTENDED

I didn't realize how much "power" I was relinquishing by forcing a state of more when it was no longer in alignment with my values. The more was so intoxicating that I would make decisions and agreements based on the win versus what aligned with my core values:

- **Integrity:** Making decisions based on what's right, not what's profitable
- **Family first:** Protecting time and energy for the people who matter most
- **Authentic success:** Building something meaningful, not just impressive
- **Service over self:** Contributing to others' growth, not just my own advancement
- **Quality over quantity:** Doing fewer things better rather than more things adequately

It was another moment of "gradually and then suddenly."

Gradually, I was veering away from these core business values. In the beginning, I could feel myself betraying them, yet after a few "wins" toward more money, promotions, and nonessentials, I became less connected to my values and ultimately experienced what felt like a sudden moment: I was so off course, I no longer recognized my goals or the results I had achieved.

## THE AVIATION TRUTH THAT CHANGED MY LIFE

You may experience this same wake-up moment where you realize you veered off course ever so slightly at one point and, over time, went off course significantly. It doesn't take much deviation from your values to throw you completely off your original path.

> If the nose of a plane is pointed only 1% off course, it will ultimately end up about 150 miles off course. Such is the case for your habits. A single poor habit, which doesn't look like much in the moment, can ultimately lead you miles off course from the direction of your goals and the life you desire.
>
> —Darren Hardy, *The Compound Effect*

This is exactly what I experienced when I veered away from my values a little at a time. I ended up with success, but my final destination was not what I originally envisioned, and it was a position of less power versus more. The dream future became more of a "nightmare" destination. Winning by diminishing your values is a definite shift in relinquishing power, not obtaining it.

## YOUR VALUES GPS CHECK

Before we can course-correct, we need to know where we are versus where we intended to be. Take this assessment right now:

**Have you relinquished power without realizing it?**

- Are you making decisions based on what looks good rather than what feels right?
- Do you say yes to opportunities that conflict with your stated priorities?

- Are you measuring success by external validation rather than internal satisfaction?

**Have you held true to your values and your vision?**

- Can you clearly articulate your top-five core values?
- Do your daily actions align with these values?
- When did you last make a decision that honored your values over immediate gain?

**Has "more" taken your power?**

- Are you busier but less fulfilled than you were five years ago?
- Do you have more possessions but less peace?
- Have you gained status but lost authenticity?

**Are you 1% off on your journey?**

- Does your current reality align with the vision you had for yourself five years ago?
- Have you reached your business goal but sacrificed your family time?
- Have you created a life that looks perfect externally, yet inside are you out of alignment?
- Have you found yourself having everything, yet having the wrong everything?

## VALUES ALIGNMENT EXERCISE

**Step 1: Identify Your Core Values.** From the following list, circle your top 10 values, then narrow to your top 5:

*Integrity, Family, Freedom, Adventure, Security,*
*Creativity, Service, Excellence, Growth, Authenticity,*
*Peace, Success, Connection, Fun, Health, Spirituality,*
*Achievement, Balance, Respect, Love, Wealth, Money*

**Your Top 5 Values:**

1. ______________________________
2. ______________________________
3. ______________________________
4. ______________________________
5. ______________________________

**Step 2: Rate Your Alignment (1–10 scale).** For each value, rate how well your current life aligns:

- Value 1: ____/10 Current alignment
- Value 2: ____/10 Current alignment
- Value 3: ____/10 Current alignment
- Value 4: ____/10 Current alignment
- Value 5: ____/10 Current alignment

**Step 3: Identify the Gaps.** Any value rated 6 or below indicates you're "off course" in that area.

Are you ready to correct your flight path?

---

## THE THREE NAVIGATION SYSTEMS: CORRECTING COURSE THROUGH LESS

How do you remove the excess and focus on the less—the fewer, highest-quality, and best things for you? It's a process. Like any aircraft correction, we need to address three critical navigation systems: *Personal Less*, *Financial Less*, and *Business Less*.

These three systems are all intertwined and influence each other. When one is off course, it affects the others. Calibrating all three is essential to reaching your intended destination.

## Navigation System 1: Personal Less—The Proximity Power

Your personal less means releasing unnecessary commitments and distractions to create space for deeper connections and a more fulfilling life. But it's not just about releasing—it's about strategically allocating your time to the right people. Your relationships can either reinforce or resist your best and highest power of alignment. In chapter 8, we'll explore how choosing fewer, deeper relationships amplifies your energy and focus.

## Navigation System 2: Financial Less—The Joy-Based Audit

My financial reality was the most challenging to wrap my brain around. What exactly would "less" mean for me, my family, and my life? Did I have to give up my salary or income to experience "less"?

Ultimately, the answer was no. It was more of a reallocation of the money I was earning. I was comfortable reading my P&L and financials and following my advisor's lead, yet I failed to look at what was being spent monthly on the "things" and assess what value they held.

Alignment is not only about aligning your values with your goals but also about who you align with in your personal life. Do not mistake similar interests for like values. Who you align with matters. The people you align with in your inner circle will have an influence on your life, business, wealth, and relationships. Time exposed with your values out of alignment may cause you to drift away from your values. Typically, if others' values are different from yours, they will pull your own values down. Rarely is it the other way around. Some signs that you may be out of alignment are that you start making excuses for the behavior of misaligned people or feel uncomfortable when in social settings with them.

Your environment becomes your thermostat. Think of it this way: You enter a conference room, and it is *freezing*. The thermostat is set to 68 degrees. Over time, you start to adjust to the temperature in the room. You may put on a jacket or move away from a vent, yet the thermostat does not change—you do. Slowly but surely, your body adjusts and the thermostat stays steady. This is exactly what happens with your environmental thermostat: It will pull you up or down.

If you are feeling off or that your relationships are less than deep, you may need to do a quick self-audit of those around you. Check in to see if they hold similar values. Do you find yourself making excuses for them? Do you feel uncomfortable or out of sorts when you are in their presence?

Like other areas of life and business, our choice of whom to have in proximity to us must be strategic. I do not hesitate to ask those I feel drawn to to share their values or perspective on life with me. What I have found is that those who are committed to their values and true to themselves can share easily and effortlessly. Those who must "think" about it are most likely trying to figure out what I want to hear or what they think they should say versus their truth.

Proximity and alignment matter!

## The Convertible Revelation

I spent 90 days assessing my true expenses, breaking them down into specifics rather than just viewing them as line items. When I honestly looked at my expenses for transportation, I realized we had a convertible that sat in our garage 90% of the time and wasn't being driven.

The convertible had moved with us from California to Austin. As you can imagine, the heat of Texas wasn't a great setting for a convertible compared to the cool Southern California weather. This was one of our lease vehicles, so we used a service to buy out our lease for a minimal fee, relieving ourselves of the monthly expense (payment, insurance, etc.).

What I found revealing was that we were carrying these expenses yet were "numb" to them, as they were just recurring payments. While we could afford them and they weren't creating hardship on our monthly cash flow, *they were no longer filling us with joy or happiness.*

## The Space Creation Effect

Part of the gift of "less" is it allows the space for other things to show up. Many times, those other things were not even on your radar screen and end up bigger than you could have imagined. The impact that "less" had was more money to do other things with—invest, donate, save, fund scholarships, help friends. But the biggest thing it did was *create space for more to come into my life.* Opportunities started to show up that seemed to appear out of nowhere. I know they were created because I finally had the space for them in my financial world.

## YOUR FINANCIAL NAVIGATION RESET: THE JOY-BASED FINANCIAL AUDIT PROCESS

**Step 1: 30-Day Complete Expense Tracking.** Track every expense for 30 days—every coffee, subscription, purchase, and payment.

**Step 2: Joy Categorization.** For each expense, assign a Joy Rating:

- **High Joy (8–10):** Brings consistent happiness, aligns with values, enhances life quality

- **Medium Joy (4–7):** Neutral feelings, mixed emotions, occasionally valuable
- **Low Joy (1–3):** Habit driven, numb, no positive feeling or active frustration

**Step 3: Elimination Strategy.**

- **Immediately eliminate:** All expenses rated 1–2
- **Evaluate for elimination:** All expenses rated 3–4
- **Keep but optimize:** All expenses rated 5–7
- **Protect and potentially increase:** All expenses rated 8–10

**Step 4: Reallocation Plan.** Take the money freed up from eliminations and allocate it as follows:

- **50%:** High Joy experiences or purchases
- **25%:** Investment/savings opportunities
- **25%:** Charitable giving that aligns with your values

**The question that will guide you:** When was the last time you did a deep dive on your finances? What could you have less of to create more space for opportunities or simply peace?

## *Navigation System 3: Business Less—The 20% Power Focus*

Many of us have so much of our value attached to our business that it becomes a significant part of our identity and lives. We use it as a measuring stick for our success and place in the business world.

Business Less is not about "resigning" from your current position. It's about focusing on your 20% (Pareto Principle), using your strengths in areas where you excel, and taking the other tasks off your plate—again, creating space for you to do other things.

## THE THINKING-TIME REVOLUTION

I remember when I was first introduced to this concept early in my coaching career. The CEO of our company encouraged each of us to have one hour a day of thinking time in our schedule. I was swimming as fast as I could; taking an entire hour to just "think" was incomprehensible.

Still, I decided to try this. My first thoughts during this "thinking time" were, "I should be doing X" or "What is the purpose of this? I have so much to do." Then I leaned into the exercise and allowed myself to assess and reflect—and reflection fuels growth. It was in this thinking time that I discovered efficiencies and low-income-earning activities that I was holding on to for the sake of being busy or feeling important.

When I leveraged those activities to others and cleared the space, I grew as a coach. I was able to prepare for my clients differently. I was able to spend time researching and collaborating with other coaches to learn new models and systems. The "less" in my business allowed the "work-on" time, which created space for massive growth and more powerful interactions with my clients.

## YOUR BUSINESS NAVIGATION CALIBRATION: THE 80/20 BUSINESS ANALYSIS

**Week 1: Activity Documentation.** Document every business activity for one full week:

- Client work
- Administrative tasks
- Meetings
- Email/communication

- Planning/strategy
- Learning/development
- Networking

**Week 2: Impact Assessment.** Rate each activity on business impact (1–10 scale):

- **9–10:** Critical activities that directly drive results and revenue
- **7–8:** Important activities that support core business functions
- **4–6:** Moderately useful activities with mixed results
- **1–3:** Low-impact activities done from habit or perceived necessity

**Week 3: The Elimination and Delegation Matrix**

- **Eliminate immediately** all activities rated 1–3.
- **Delegate or systematize** activities rated 4–6 that others can do.
- **Optimize** activities rated 7–8 to make them more efficient.
- **Protect and expand** activities rated 9–10 to become your nonnegotiable focus.

**Week 4: Implementation and Thinking Time**

- Implement your new activity focus
- Protect one hour daily for strategic thinking
- Use reclaimed time for high-impact activities only

## THE 30-DAY FLIGHT PLAN: COURSE-CORRECTION SPRINT

Why 30 days? Because work *expands* to the time allowed! This is one of my favorite universal truths. Parkinson's Law identified this truth through the story of a woman whose only task in a day was to send a postcard—a task that would take a busy person approximately three minutes. But the woman spent an hour finding the card, another half hour looking for her glasses, 90 minutes writing the card, 20 minutes deciding whether to take an umbrella on her walk to the mailbox . . . and on and on until her day was filled.[24] Can you relate?

If we gave ourselves 365 days to complete the "less" task, I promise you it would take longer than truly necessary. Thirty days creates the perfect window. It takes away the belief that you have plenty of time to complete the task while providing enough time to build lasting change.

I have my clients work in 30-day sprints because it turns big goals into focused, doable actions. When you have a clear path, a strategic plan, and a tight timeline—you become unstoppable.

Think about the day before you leave for vacation. You're a force of nature. Focused. Efficient. Getting things done like your life depends on it. Why? Because you know there's no time to waste. That's Parkinson's Law in action: The task expands to fit the time you give it. When the time is limited, magic happens.

That same energy—that sense of urgency and clarity—is exactly what fuels a 30-day sprint. When you commit fully for just one month, you'll be amazed by what you can accomplish.

## YOUR COMPLETE 30-DAY COURSE-CORRECTION PLAN

### Preflight Week: Goal Selection and Planning

Choose *one* primary goal for your sprint—personal, financial, or business improvement. Break that goal down into specific, measurable outcomes and map out the strategies necessary to achieve it.

**Goal-Setting Framework**

1. **Select your primary focus area:** Personal Less, Financial Less, or Business Less.
2. **Define your specific 30-day outcome:** What will be different at the end?
3. **Identify your key strategies:** What are the three to five main actions required?
4. **Create your weekly milestones:** What will you accomplish each week?
5. **Design your daily actions:** What will you do each day to stay on track?

## Week 1: Navigation System Calibration

**Days 1–3:** Complete your chosen audit (Relationship Energy, Joy-Based Financial, or 80/20 Business).

**Days 4–5:** Analyze results and identify opportunities.

**Days 6–7:** Create your elimination and optimization plan.

## Week 2: Course-Correction Implementation

**Days 8–14:** Begin implementing your elimination plan.

- Start saying no to low-value commitments.
- Cancel Low Joy financial commitments.
- Delegate or eliminate low-impact business activities.
- Track your progress daily.

## Week 3: New Flight Path Optimization

**Days 15–21:** Double down on high-value activities.

- Invest more time in your Front Row relationships (see chapter 8).
- Reallocate financial resources to High Joy priorities.
- Focus exclusively on your 20% business activities.
- Protect your new boundaries.

### Week 4: Integration and Sustainability

**Days 22–30:** Lock in your new operating system.

- Create systems to maintain your new priorities.
- Build accountability measures for staying on course.
- Plan your next 30-day sprint.
- Celebrate your transformation.

---

## HANDLING TURBULENCE: THE THOUGHT NAVIGATION SYSTEM

During your 30-day sprint, you'll face disempowering thoughts that will try to sabotage your results. Remember, thoughts drive all results, and until we process and change them, they will continue to create doubt.

When you notice negative or disempowering thoughts arising, use this navigation system:

**Current Disempowering Thought:** ________________________

**Feelings/Emotions/Energy:** ________________________

**Actions/Inaction:** ________________________

**Predicted Results:** ________________________

**Apply Byron Katie's Four Questions:**

1. Is it true? ____________________
2. Can you absolutely know it is true? ____________________
3. How do you react when you believe that thought? ____________________
4. Who would you be without the thought? ____________________

**Turn it around: Your new empowering thought:** ____________________

**Run the new thought through the reTHINK Thought Flow Model:**

**Thought (new):** ____________________

**Feelings/Emotions/Energy:** ____________________

**Actions:** ____________________

**Predicted Results:** ____________________

You'll notice a shift in your energy and beliefs because you've changed the thought pattern. This new thought can carry you forward, though the "old thought" may bubble up again. Just reflect on the model with the new thought and lean into the flow.

## LANDING AT YOUR INTENDED DESTINATION: THE POWER OF FOCUS

Small course corrections lead to dramatically different destinations. The power of less is greater than you have ever considered. Stepping into the space of less for Personal, Financial, and Business holds tremendous power. It helps clear the noise and allows space for great things to emerge.

When I adopted these tactics in my business, it was beyond noticeable. It was as if I took a blurry vision and put it into focus. The colors were more vibrant, the shapes more defined, and the clarity was beyond anything I had ever experienced before. It was as if someone turned a light on in my world that had been on a dimmer switch and only operating at 25%.

The transformation was immediate and comprehensive:

- It lightened the load of my schedule and made my remaining commitments more meaningful.
- Time with my family and friends became more focused, and I was incredibly present.
- Meetings and work tasks became more focused—I was truly present for the first time in a long time.
- I wasn't consumed with rushing from one meeting to the next.
- I could feel a stronger connection in everything I did.

As a mentor of mine has said over and over, "Be where your feet are." For the first time, my mind, focus, and attention were exactly where my feet were. If you were in front of me, you were getting 100% of my attention, not just a portion of it. I realized that those in my presence were feeling seen and heard—some of them for the first time in a long time. It was a huge gift to give to them, but even more so for me.

## YOUR FLIGHT PLAN SUMMARY

You now have the complete navigation system for course correction:

1. **Your Values GPS:** Know where you're supposed to be going.
2. **The Three Navigation Systems:** Personal, Financial, and Business Less.

3. **The 30-Day Sprint Plan:** Your structured course-correction process.
4. **The Thought Navigation System:** Tools to handle mental turbulence.

The question is not whether this approach works. Instead, it is whether you're ready to commit to the course correction. That, and also: *When will you be where your feet are?* Think about it.

The beauty in this journey is the clarity that will come from doing the work—when you know the truth and have clarity. The power lies in the decision to make different choices. To take your new awareness and lean into the discomfort of change and trust in the path that is unfolding.

Take the 30-day sprint and feel the changes happen! You can do anything for 30 days, and the impact on your life, business, and relationships will be difficult to ignore. The change and awareness will motivate you to continue the learnings and changes.

In the next chapter, we'll take these Less Over More navigation principles and apply them specifically to clearing the professional clutter that's blocking your business or career breakthrough. We'll discover how the "necessary clearing" creates space for growth opportunities you never saw coming.

## LESS OVER MORE: KEY INSIGHTS

- **The 1% Problem:** Small deviations from your values compound over time, taking you to completely different destinations than intended.
- **Less creates focus and leverage:** The more focused energy you put on fewer things, the more powerful your results become.
- **Three Navigation Systems:** Personal Less (relationships), Financial Less (expenses), and Business Less (activities) all work together to keep you on course.
- **The 30-Day Sprint Method:** Concentrated focus over one month creates more lasting change than scattered effort over a year.
- **Be where your feet are:** True presence and focused attention become your greatest gifts to yourself and others.

# CHAPTER 7

# WHEN MORE BLOCKS FUTURE OPPORTUNITIES

Here's a truth that might sting a little: More can be the greatest thief of future opportunities. Not because opportunities aren't coming your way, but because you've left no space for them to land.

Picture yourself at a holiday dinner, laser focused on the "big" meal. Maybe you've even skipped breakfast and lunch, saving every bit of appetite for this moment. You approach the buffet like a strategic mission, piling your plate with layers of special holiday foods until you can't see the surface anymore. Gravy threatens to spill over the edges of your plate. It is a monument to abundance.

Then, just as you sit down to enjoy your well-deserved feast, the host announces they forgot to bring out two dishes—and they're both things you absolutely love. But there's zero space left on your plate. You've blocked yourself from receiving what you couldn't see coming.

This is exactly how it works in business and life. You fill your days and your life with so much "more" that when real blessings and opportunities arrive, there's simply no room. The question isn't whether these opportunities go to someone else; it's whether you've created space to even recognize them when they appear.

## DID WE BUILD OUR OWN DAM?

Beavers build dams for protection from predators and to create stable environments for their lodges and food storage. You could call a dam just a "clog" in the river, but for beavers, it serves a vital purpose. They can build their dam in less than 24 hours when needed.

We humans also build dams, but ours take weeks, months, years, even decades to construct. Layer by layer, we work diligently to pile up our "more"—jobs, houses, cars, designer bags, titles, salaries. We build these external symbols believing they're protecting us, moving us forward, or creating safety.

But unlike the beaver's dam, which actually serves its purpose, our dam often blocks the very opportunities we're seeking while providing only false protection. We've clogged our own flow.

Are you ready to disassemble your dam? Are you ready to bring flow back into your life and business by clearing the "more" that's blocking you?

## THE GPS FOR YOUR LIFE'S WORK: FINDING YOUR WHY

I believe we busy ourselves with more to feel better or worthy about our position in business and life. Sometimes we do it because we've lost our way regarding our original goals and vision. We get "seduced" by opportunities for more and pivot without even knowing we've done it.

This happens so gradually that we don't notice we're off course. The solution? Get crystal clear on your Why—your true north.

Without a clear Why, we're apt to get distracted or lost. Think of your Why as your GPS. When we drive to a new destination without GPS or a map, we might never arrive. We get lost, and maybe settle for something else because we became distracted. But when we plug in our coordinates and know exactly where we're going, GPS gives us a 99% chance of arriving. It allows us to focus and trust.

## MY WHY JOURNEY

I struggled with identifying my Why for years. I heard it discussed at conferences and training sessions, even by my coach, yet it remained elusive. I read the books, did the work, but nothing felt congruent.

Part of my struggle was rooted in how I was raised. I was taught to be humble and modest, not to set visions or goals so big that failure would bring great disappointment. We were not a risk-taking family. Our approach was to do what we could, give our best, and accept what was given. You took the path provided rather than creating your own. Setting a Why felt risky—not something we ever did.

My breakthrough came when I started incorporating others into my vision. Though still rooted in my Why, I carved out space to pour into four areas that matter most: myself, my family and friends, my team, and my legacy. These are the sources of my greatest energy and inspiration. When I focused just on the "me" portion of the Why, missing the goal or giving up only affected me. In fact, I rarely shared my Why with anyone. The new approach includes others, and I share my Why with those who would be impacted by my vision. Knowing others are affected by my actions and accomplishments is a true driver for me.

## CREATING YOUR WHY: A PRACTICAL APPROACH

Let's create your Why right now. Start with your three-year vision:

**Step 1: Envision Without Limits:** Don't get wrapped up in the "how." Let yourself imagine what your life and business could look like in three years—health, relationships, income, wealth, experiences. If you start venturing into "how," stop and just enjoy the possibility.

**Step 2: Sit in Success:** Imagine you've achieved those goals. Let yourself experience the emotions that come with that success.

**Step 3: Write Your Success Letter:** Write a letter to yourself dated three years from now. Make it specific and clear. Write as if the events have happened, not "When I accomplish X, I will feel . . ." Include the impact these goals have had on yourself, your family and friends, your team, and your legacy.

*Example: "Today is December 31, 2028. I am so grateful for the life and business I have created. Looking at my savings account balance of $2,500,000 gives me such peace. I'm signing the last of the bonus checks for my team—the pride I have for their accomplishments is beyond anything I imagined. I'm excited to give my family their passports for our dream European vacation, knowing I've paid for it in full and the memories we'll create . . ."*

Truly spend time on this exercise as the impact is beyond measure. For some this may be a challenge to "daydream" your future. To allow yourself to think big and to give yourself permission to experience the joys of success. The impact happens simply because your brain (unconscious mind) cannot tell the difference between real and "make-believe." It views your vision of the future as the truth! Once your brain views this as "done," it starts assisting you on the "how" of getting to the vision it sees as your truth. Plus, it feels really good to sit in the potential and experience the emotion of your future success. The emotional aspect of this exercise is significant in motivating you to take action.

**Step 4: Create Your One-Year Vision:** Repeat this process for your one-year goals.

**Step 5: Keep It Close:** Keep your Why with you at all times. There will be moments when you're tempted to stray from what's important. When you see what's at risk if you step out of flow, it will put you back on track quickly.

## VALUES: YOUR BUSINESS COMPASS

Beyond your Why, you need clarity on your values—not just moral values, but your core business values. I know my top three values and their order of importance (Fun, Freedom, and Financial Abundance). Until we're aware of these and operate within them, we're susceptible to going off course and being tricked into "more."

Having abundant clarity on my values allows me to make critical decisions with certainty. If a decision goes against my values, it's an easy no. Without knowing these values, you're saying yes or no based on impulse or the potential for more, rather than congruence with your truth.

## A COSTLY LESSON

Years ago, I decided to go into business with "friends." The potential was intoxicating. All I could see was massive success and fortune—at least, that's what I was being told. I said yes while everything inside me was screaming NO.

Had I taken a moment to review my top values, the "no" would have been so much easier. As I mentioned, my top business values are Fun, Freedom, and Financial Abundance. This opportunity offered none of these. The personalities involved didn't allow for fun or freedom, and while financial success was possible, early indicators showed the vision wasn't coming to life.

About 90 days in, I knew I'd made the wrong choice. I was completely out of sync and feeling off. Through a series of events, I finally looked at my values and made the decision to dissolve the partnership. It wasn't easy, but as soon as I made that decision, I felt my energy return. The wave of relief was massive, and success was right around the corner. It truly was as if the lid of my success jar had been removed! Friends, colleagues, clients, and people I did not know all started reaching out to me, inquiring about coaching and programs and the new company. The opening created by ending that partnership opened up my "success portal" and opportunity after opportunity showed up. Was I scared at first? *Yes!* Was it one of the best decisions ever made? *Yes!*

## THE POWER OF NO

One of my favorite sayings is, "When you say yes to one thing, you are saying no to something else." How many times have you said yes to something and within hours or days regretted that quick response?

Yes is one of the major contributors to "the clog." We feel obligated to say yes—to employers, clients, friends, spouses, or opportunities. We've been conditioned to believe that no feels like rejection. We don't want to let anyone down, plus we like the gratification that comes from saying yes.

Sometimes we say yes because of our ego. We get caught up in the image or position and how important it will sound. We might say yes because we don't want someone else to move ahead of us. Our ego plays interesting games.

## REFRAMING NO

We need to reframe our story around the word no. It's not rejection—it's taking a stand for yourself, your vision, and your values. Saying no is aligning your truest self with actions and activities that lift you. Think of no as your greatest protector and supporter.

My old self struggled tremendously with saying no. I was afraid of hurting feelings or being overlooked for future opportunities. The truth was, some of the people I was saying yes to were benefiting while I unconsciously sabotaged my vision and values.

## LEARNING TO SAY NO GRACEFULLY

I started observing successful people and noticed a pattern in how they said no. There wasn't a lot of explaining—just simple statements without emotion, charge, or rationalization. The receiver of "no" wasn't devastated. This discovery was a gift.

Here are some effective ways to say no kindly:

- "Thank you for thinking of me. I'm unable to participate at this time."
- "I have other commitments and am unable to take this on."
- "My schedule is full right now, and I can't give this the attention it deserves. I appreciate you thinking of me."
- "Thank you for the opportunity. It sounds wonderful, and I need to pass."

## WHEN NO ISN'T ALWAYS AN OPTION

Sometimes you simply can't say no—deadlines shift, or you're the only person with the needed skill set. Often, our hesitation to say no stems from what I call the "superhero effect." By agreeing to help, you feel like you're saving the day, which triggers a dopamine release. Your mind may crave this experience and continue seeking more "yeses."

If this sounds familiar, try this: Before automatically saying yes, pause and say, "Let me check a few things before I commit." This buys you time to assess whether the yes is out of habit and whether the proposition aligns with your values.

## THE VALUES CALENDAR TEST

If you've never been consciously aware of your values before, let's see how aligned your current life is with them:

- Grab your calendar and three highlighters (green, yellow, blue).
    - Green = Important and aligned with your values
    - Yellow = Important but not aligned with your values
    - Blue = Not important and not aligned with your values
- Review your last two months and highlight each activity accordingly.

This exercise reveals where you're spending time on tasks that don't support your highest good. It's often eye opening to see how much yellow and blue fill your calendar.

## WHEN WE LOSE OUR WAY

I've always believed that life provides opportunities when you're ready to receive them. Part of being ready means not clogging the way with excess "more." Sometimes we get so far off course and so saturated with "more" that what we truly want can't find its way to us.

If you feel stuck or clogged, it may be time to revisit your original goals and vision. We often stray from our path gradually, distracted by the allure of more. What I've found with clients who come to me feeling clogged is that they have written plans and visions, but what they're actually doing doesn't match what they wrote. They create fabulous plans, tuck them away in a drawer or electronic file, and get busy doing something else entirely, usually falling back to old behaviors that feel comfortable and familiar.

## MY OWN CLOG

My most recent encounter with getting clogged happened during my contract with a large coaching company. I started with a specific vision: to be a coach who helped anyone with the desire to be successful grow their business and lives. This simple goal was the fire that pushed me through challenges and allowed me to move forward even when things seemed impossible.

At some point, I saw an elevated coaching position in the company. Each coach in this position appeared to be doing very well financially and living big lives. I started shifting my attention to that role—for the money and attention. I said yes to different training programs to position myself for one of these coveted spots. I had created a story around what that position was and the amazing opportunity that I believed it would create.

Sadly, I was doing it for the wrong reasons. My original vision was about helping others succeed. This new goal was all about me and my finances. When I thought about the position, I didn't think about my impact on others based upon my values—I was too busy imagining my big life.

I lost sight of my vision without being consciously aware of it. When we don't regularly reflect on our true path, and when we're unclear on our values, our minds allow us to drift.

## FLOW AND ALIGNMENT: COMING HOME TO YOURSELF

When was the last time you felt genuinely aligned with your vision and values? What was happening at that time? Can you duplicate that feeling again?

Alignment feels like coming home to yourself. When you're aligned, decisions become easier, energy flows naturally, and opportunities seem to appear effortlessly. This isn't magic; it's simply what happens when you remove the clogs and create space for what truly matters.

Start aligning your vision, your Why, and your values, and you'll feel a sense of clarity like never before. You'll loosen the grip of "more" and feel the blockages breaking up. Keep in mind, you may need to involve others in this process, and you'll need patience. It didn't take one day to get clogged, and it may take time to restore the flow.

Trust the process. Once you begin, you'll start to feel the energy shift and changes coming. Embrace the possibility and enjoy the journey to creating a clearer path for success. So much is waiting for you on the other side of more.

Remember the dinner plate metaphor. Instead of piling more and more onto your plate until nothing else can fit, leave space. Create room for the unexpected delights, the opportunities you can't yet see, the blessings that want to find their way to you.

The art isn't in accumulating more—it's in creating space to receive what matters most. When you unclog your life from unnecessary "more," you don't just make room for opportunities. You make room for joy, peace, meaningful relationships, and the deep satisfaction that comes from living in alignment with your truest self.

That's when the magic happens. That's when less becomes infinitely more.

## LESS OVER MORE: KEY INSIGHTS

- **Leave space on your plate**: More can block future opportunities. Create room to receive what you can't yet see coming.
- **Your Why is your GPS**: A clear, emotionally connected Why that includes others keeps you on track when distractions try to pull you off course.
- **Values make decisions easy**: Know your top three values and use them as your decision filter. If something doesn't align with them, it's a clear no.
- **No is your protector**: Saying no to what doesn't support you is saying yes to what matters most—it's not rejection, it's alignment.
- **Alignment creates flow**: When your actions match your Why and values, opportunities appear effortlessly and energy flows naturally.

CHAPTER 8

# FEWER, DEEPER RELATIONSHIPS AND THE SCIENCE OF A GOOD LIFE

One way I used to measure my worth was by the size of my social circle. At any given moment, I had a massive list of people I could call for drinks, dinner, or shared holidays. It was a tremendous ego boost knowing I had so many connections and "friends." I was collecting relationships like trophies, believing that more friends meant I was more valuable as a person.

Then came the awakening. It was a slow wave that caught my attention and then escalated, like a bucket of ice water dumped over my head. I began noticing something I couldn't ignore: After spending time with certain friends, I felt drained. These interactions left negative imprints on my mindset, energy, and thoughts that lingered long after we parted ways. Conversations with them focused on everything that could go wrong, potential problems, and worst-case scenarios. There was no celebration of success or excitement about future opportunities. I found myself starting to focus on the negative aspects of my own life, and then things that once held no power over me suddenly did.

Then there were other friends who made me feel empowered, positive, and like anything I desired was possible. They shared exciting news about future projects, amazing trips, and incredible opportunities. They were as excited about my successes as I was, sometimes even more so, without a hint of jealousy or envy. After spending time with them, I felt energized and saw the good in my life and business.

That's when I realized T. Harv Eker, author of *Secrets of the Millionaire Mind* and a leading voice on how beliefs and focus shape financial and personal success, was right: "What you focus on expands."[25] With the negative group, I was focusing on problems, and that energy was expanding into every area of my life. With the positive group, the opposite was true. I began calling it the "contagion effect"—their energy was literally contagious.

As in all areas of life, Pareto's 80/20 rule was in full effect. The majority of my "friends" (80%) fell into the negative, depleting category, while only a small portion (20%) were positive and uplifting. This meant the negative interactions were consuming most of my time and headspace, having a far greater impact on my life and business than I'd ever imagined.

Once this awakening happened, everything changed. I made the decision to stop investing time with the negative influences and start focusing on those who made a positive difference. I began the clearing—no more collecting friends for the sake of having them or out of obligation. I was going to reduce the clutter and focus on fewer, higher-quality relationships.

That one decision changed how I experienced life and business. Little did I know it would also impact my health, success, and happiness in ways the science of relationships proves time and time again.

## THE SCIENCE: WHY RELATIONSHIPS DETERMINE EVERYTHING

Strong and meaningful relationships aren't just nice to have—they're the foundation of a long, healthy, and fulfilling life. The benefit goes far beyond what most of us consider, and it's an area we must pay attention to as we craft our desired lives.

Harvard's Longevity Study, which began in 1938 and continues today, has revealed some stunning insights about the power of relationships. The study's key findings show that social connections are vital to both mental and physical health. People who are more socially connected to family, friends, and community are happier, physically healthier, and live longer. Your mind and body are deeply interconnected in ways we're only beginning to understand. Would you ever have connected the impact of relationships on your physical and mental health along with your longevity?

On the flip side, people who are more isolated tend to be less happy, experience earlier health declines, have decreased brain function, and live shorter lives. But here's the crucial insight: It's not about the number of relationships you have—it's about the quality. A statistic that stopped me in my tracks is that loneliness is as harmful as smoking 15 cigarettes per day, according to a study led by Dr. Julianne Holt-Lunstad.[26]

Living in the midst of conflict is detrimental to health, while warm and healthy relationships are protective. Strong relationships don't just benefit physical health; they protect cognitive function, helping to delay mental decline and sharpen memory in later life. The study emphasizes that "social fitness" is as important as physical fitness, requiring us to actively nurture our connections.

Perhaps most importantly, relationships act as stress regulators. Close relationships help the body manage stress and recover from challenging events.

## THE MODERN CHALLENGE: DISCONNECTED THROUGH CONNECTION

Here's the paradox of our time: We have more ways to connect than ever before, yet loneliness has reached epidemic proportions. How can we feel so disconnected when technology promises to bring us closer together—when it literally puts "connection" at our fingertips?

When I first signed up for social media, the feeling of connection was incredibly exciting. I could reconnect with old classmates, distant friends, and people I rarely saw in person. Initially, I spent maybe 30 minutes a day on these platforms. Then things changed. Gradually, then suddenly, I went from brief check-ins to finding myself logged in for hours.

What I didn't realize was how this was affecting my life outside the screen—what I was missing in the real world. My smartphone became a gateway I could access anytime, anywhere. I found myself checking in while driving, while working, during any downtime. It became one of the first things I checked when I woke up and the last thing I did before bed.

What started as a simple connection to the outside world had replaced real, in-person interactions. My skill at the art of human connection was diminishing, and I wasn't even aware it was happening.

Bestselling author Noreena Hertz, in her book *The Lonely Century*, argues that we're facing a rising epidemic of loneliness in the 21st century—a crisis with social, economic, and political dimensions. She connects this loneliness to changes in technology, workplace structures, and society that have led to increased isolation and disconnection. Loneliness isn't just a personal feeling; it's a systemic issue impacting our health, economics, and democracy.

Think about how rapidly things have changed in the last decade. Technology allows us to work from anywhere, eliminating the natural social interactions that come from shared workspaces. Many of my lifelong friendships formed because we came to a central location and worked together, spending significant time face-to-face and truly getting to know each other. I was exposed to different points of view and ideas, creating a strong sense of community and belonging.

Author Robert Putnam's research on social connectedness in his book *Bowling Alone* shows that Americans have become increasingly isolated from each other and their communities. Overall participation in organized group activities has decreased while pursuit of individualistic leisure activities has increased. We're retreating and functioning alone more than we are as a community, conditioning ourselves to prefer isolation over connection.

The replacement of real relationships with online connections can be more costly than we think. While social media makes us feel connected to someone's life, we're only seeing a carefully curated highlight reel. Rarely does someone post their mistakes, disappointments, or failures publicly. We end up comparing our real-life struggles to others' edited versions of success, creating an environment of comparison and judgment that isolates us further.

## THE TRUE COST: WHEN WEAK RELATIONSHIPS DRAIN LIFE

It's crucial to understand that weak relationships don't just lack depth—they actively take a toll on our emotional and physical health. Research from experts like Dr. John Gottman and Harvard's happiness studies reveals the hidden costs of emotionally disconnected relationships.

Regarding emotions, weak relationships create chronic stress and anxiety. Constant tension, distrust, or emotional instability leads to a feeling of walking on eggshells. Over time, if you don't feel valued or respected, you begin to internalize that message, leading to low self-worth and diminished confidence.

Weak relationships are also emotionally exhausting. You are constantly giving more than you receive and/or living in "repair and fix" mode, which completely depletes your emotional energy. You may feel resentful, exhausted, or like you've lost yourself in the relationship. Perhaps most telling, you can feel profoundly lonely while being surrounded by people—feeling unseen, unheard, or misunderstood can be more isolating than truly being alone.

The physical impact is equally serious. Stress from weak relationships can cause sleep deprivation, insomnia, or nightmares. When emotional safety is lacking, your nervous system can't fully relax. Toxic social connections activate your body's stress response, leading to increased cortisol levels. Prolonged exposure to high cortisol causes inflammation, weight gain, hypertension, and a compromised immune system, leading to slower recovery from illness or injury.

Physical symptoms like headaches, stomach issues, body aches, and fatigue are common when your emotional state is disrupted. The body often manifests what the mind is suppressing, and consistent emotional distress likewise dampens immune resilience.

The ultimate cost goes beyond health. Weak relationships rob you of clarity—you spend so much time second-guessing, analyzing, or replaying scenarios that you can't focus on yourself or your goals. Your energy, creativity, motivation, and productivity suffer. When you're in emotional survival mode, personal and professional growth becomes nearly impossible.

The impact of weak relationships often unfolds gradually, then suddenly. What begins as small emotional or physical strains slowly erodes your well-being, and if left unchecked, the long-term effects can be deeply damaging.

## THE 25-FOOT RULE THAT CHANGES EVERYTHING

The Kellogg School of Management discovered something remarkable about proximity. Research published in 2017 demonstrated that coworkers within a 25-foot radius of high-performing employees experienced a 15% performance boost, translating to an additional $1 million in annual profits.[27]

But here's the critical insight: If you are within a 25-foot radius of low-performing employees, you can experience a 30% decline in your performance. The power of proximity is critical, and who you associate and collaborate with matters.

If proximity can have this significant of an impact in your work life, it can also affect your friends and personal life. Remember, how you do one thing is how you do everything. If this impact is present at work, it can also be present in your personal life.

## THE SOLUTION: CURATING YOUR "FRONT ROW"

If you're ready to embrace the "less" of friendships and focus on meaningful, healthy connections, there is a solution. Like all important changes, it requires intentional actions and commitment to a different approach.

I started the process of crafting my front row of friends over a decade ago. I consider my front row friends to be the ones that have the most profound and positive impact on my life in all areas. I think of them as the people who are sitting in the front row of my auditorium. The ones who will cheer me on, encourage me, and celebrate my wins with me.

To begin this process, I had to treat this like other strategies in my life and business. I had to do a deep dive on how I would successfully protect the space of my front row as a place of power.

I am fundamentally aware that how we communicate and stay in touch with our friends has changed over the past decade; yet, for me, connection to my front row is imperative. I realized, though, that I had to do an audit in all areas where I was communicating and connecting with others.

## THE SOCIAL MEDIA REALITY CHECK

I was confident about my social media discipline. My social media was a combination of connections to people I know and a marketing tool for my business. I assumed I had this part of my life under control. Man, was I wrong. Not just wrong, but really, really wrong.

I downloaded an app that tracks platform visits and time spent. I set limits of five visits per day with seven minutes of active time. To my horror, I exceeded those limits before noon on the first day. I realized I was popping on for business and then going down the rabbit hole of endless scrolling.

The app created awareness, but I had to make the commitment to honor the constraints. Since doing so, I've noticed a substantial difference in my use of time and the impact on my mindset. My highest-value friends don't live on a platform—they're in my world through face-to-face meetings, social events, work functions, and meaningful long-distance communication.

Think of social media limits as Ozempic for your digital life—reducing the burden of platforms that aren't enhancing your life can be extremely empowering. Start by limiting your social media check-ins to five times a day or less.

## THE ENERGY ASSESSMENT

Also, pay attention to how you feel during and after interactions with different friends. This was one of the simplest "tests" I used when editing my friend list and assembling my front row. If I felt depleted or devoid of energy after an encounter, I realized that person was a taker who didn't enhance my life experience.

In addition to the Kellogg School of Business statistics on the effect of being near productive people, Jim Rohn, a self-development philosopher known for emphasizing the influence of social environment and behavioral modeling on individual outcomes, noted that you become the average of the five people you spend the most time with. Who are your five? Are they who you want to be like? Do their qualities match what you want in your life? Do you aspire to be just like them?

## THE CURATION PROCESS

When I set out to choose my front row, I had to get over the guilt of not including everyone. I didn't discard those who weren't in my top tier—I simply chose to decrease the time I spent with them. I came to terms with the fact that this wasn't selfish; it was necessary. Being intentional in all other areas of my life and business meant I needed to be intentional about relationships too.

Be present where your feet are. When I was accumulating friends without intention, I wasn't always present during interactions. I'd answer texts, emails, and notifications instead of being fully engaged. This should have been a sign that the relationship wasn't high on my value chain.

I now practice being fully present during my interactions. I want to squeeze every bit of life I can from time spent with someone. By doing this, my relationships have transformed. People share more with me, and in return, they've created space for me to share at a very deep level. The essence of my friendships has changed, and I'm forever grateful.

## SETTING STANDARDS AND BOUNDARIES

You must have standards and boundaries in your friendships and clarity about what you will and won't allow. This isn't selfish; it's actually selfless because it creates a win-win situation where both people have the opportunity to grow from clear expectations.

Ask yourself: Does this person give energy or take it? Do they inspire me or drain me? When I spend time with them, do I become a better version of myself, or do I feel diminished?

## THE RESULT: LIFE WITH QUALITY RELATIONSHIPS

My current circle of friends is an amazing group of people. They are my "ride or die" peeps, the folks I'm taking with me on the journey, and vice versa. While the quantity in my front row has decreased dramatically, the quality and experiences are utterly incredible. I'm surrounded by positive, forward-thinking people. I can count on every conversation having an element of future focus—upcoming projects, trips, experiences, opportunities.

My friends are also my cheerleaders. We all share genuine happiness for each other's successes, and it feels outstanding to have people who are sincerely happy for my wins, sometimes even more than I am for myself.

A vital byproduct of these powerful friendships is the willingness to help each other win. One of the best examples is my friend Suzanne. We met at a dinner years ago and connected immediately. Our conversation was electric, each of us sharing enough of our past to get to understand each other and, most importantly, our futures. My gut was telling me that she needed to be part of my intentionally curated group of friends, and I was not wrong! From our very similar upbringing to our views on living a *huge* life, we were in alignment, lighting up when we shared our future vision with each other, along with the values we hold dear.

To this day, every conversation with Suzanne is full of future opportunities. She has helped connect me with people who can support my vision, and I've done the same for her. In fact, this book wouldn't exist without Suzanne. After many of my keynote speeches, people asked if I had a book. I mentioned this to Suzanne, and she questioned me as to why I hadn't written a book yet. To be honest, I'd considered it but never moved forward. For months, Suzanne kept encouraging me to write one, pointing out how much it could help others. When I finally agreed, she introduced me to my agent. This is what happens when you surround yourself with the right people—not because you expect to get something, but because you're with people who lift, encourage, and nudge you to be the best version of yourself.

To be clear, not every conversation with my core group is all sunshine and rainbows—there are moments when life gets challenging. But if one of us gets down or derailed, I know anyone in my group can lift them out of that place quickly. We all take this responsibility seriously and honor it.

Does your collection of friends need some adjusting? Are you ready to clear the space of "more" and move toward "less" in the friend arena? You cannot be the best version of yourself if you're constantly being pulled down or backward, if you're the only one creating energy of possibility.

Take a moment to assess your friendships and put a plan in place to pursue less. Your life and business will be enhanced. As with other areas of clearing the more, you'll be amazed at who shows up. Had I not created space in my life for quality friends, I don't believe certain key people would have appeared—I wouldn't have had room. The lesson here? Make room for your quality relationships. They will change your life entirely.

## LESS OVER MORE—FRIENDSHIP IMPACT

Here's the process I used when curating my front row. I didn't want to hurt or lose friends, so I acted with care. The prospect of setting myself up for amazing success, however, helped me get comfortable with sifting and sorting. I created three layers that helped me correctly categorize where existing and new connections belonged.

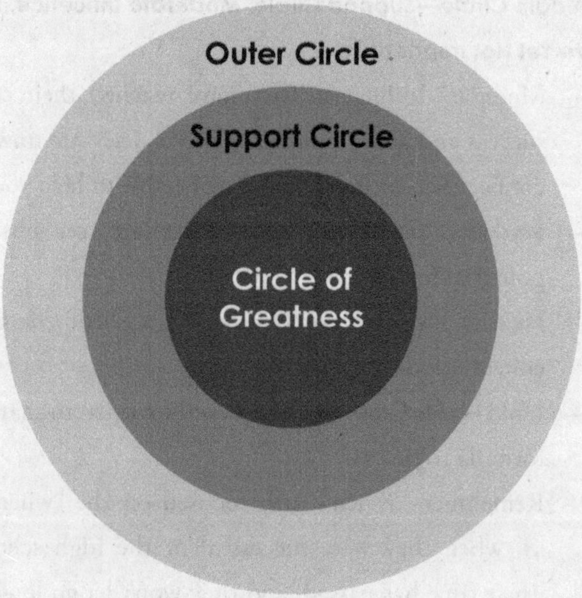


- **Front Row—Circle of Greatness: Your Source of Energy, Value, and Inspiration**
  - — Forward Thinkers
  - — Positive Focus: Uplifting, no gossiping, no living in the past, no should-have, could-have, would-have. Sees the opportunities versus obstacles.
  - — Connectors: Always willing to connect me to others who can help move my projects or life forward. Excited to bring people together to help them succeed.
  - — Sharer: Sharing best practices and opportunities they have created or implemented (investments, programs, people, systems)
  - — Energy Givers: Bring their best to the conversation. Willing to lend you their beliefs and empower you to do amazing things. Create a shield of invincibility for you to protect yourself with moving forward.

- **Middle Circle—Support Circle: Moderate Influence, Supportive Yet Not Impactful**
  - Moderate Influence: They have reached their ceiling of success and are not pursuing more. They are unwilling to connect you to those who may be able to help you.
  - Settled: Comfortable where they are, see obstacles as potential failures.
  - Neither Negative nor Positive: Bring little energy to the conversations.
  - Hold Cards Close to Their Vest: Not open to sharing their formula to success.
  - Remember "When": Stay focused on the "when"—such as, when they were successful or the high school hero. Their time has passed, and they won't let go long enough to create new success.
- **Outer Circle—Noise Zone: Distractors, the Misery Loves Company Group**
  - Gossipy: Talk about people and their failures or disappointments.
  - Stuck in the Past: Only focus is on past experiences.
  - Repeaters: Same story over and over.
  - Energy Vampire: Drain the energy from you. Conversation "hogs" that make it all about them and all the unfairness they have experienced.
  - Finger Pointer: Never their fault, always someone else causing their limits.

Remember, the key is Less Over More. Less quantity of highest impact. To organize from most impactful to least. Our goal is a minimum of 5-core in your Circle of Greatness. You may have a few more; if you have less, use this as an opportunity to create relationships with the "right more" people. Become intentional about building relationships.

## DO THE WORK

- Take out a piece of paper and list each and every friend you give time to, whether in person, via phone, texting, social media, etc.
- Categorize each person as "Front Row—Circle of Greatness," "Support Circle," or "Outer Circle."
  - — Do not judge or attempt to justify any ranking. Go with your gut and label immediately.
- Identify who you spend or give the most amount of time to.
  - — Which circle are they in?
  - — How many are in each circle?
  - — Who earns the right to your Front Row?
- Create a plan to spend more time with your Front Row.
  - — Implement a strategic plan to organize your time by circle.
  - — Create a script that you will use to turn down offers from your Support Circle and Outer Circle friends.
- Show yourself grace in putting yourself first and becoming intentional with your time.
- Do you have your five identified for your "Front Row"?
  - — Create a strategy of how and where you can grow or meet people to add to your 5-core.
- Who do you need to become to maintain your "Circle of Greatness" and to be part of someone else's "Circle of Greatness"?
  - — Less gossipy?

— More giving of resources?
— Someone who regularly dismisses obstacles and creates opportunities?

---

I know this to be true: The moment I allowed myself to be a priority and become the person that I would want to be in my "Circle of Greatness," my life changed.

This small yet powerful change impacts the way you experience life and success in profound ways. (The little things are the *big* things.) When you make the commitment to reduce your accumulation of acquaintances (friends) and become purposeful, the growth of the experience you can call upon is exponential.

What I have found is that when I adopted this change, I also started to feel the natural drift of those not in my Front Row or Support Circle friends. I realized that in some way, I was also giving them a gift. I had stopped making them uncomfortable or feeling out of place in my presence due to my commitment to be my truest self at *all* times. I no longer participated in conversation that was limiting or inappropriate (gossip) and that actually made them feel awkward and at times frustrated. My deciding to limit exposure was a win for both of us. As a result, the space the outer two circles held shrank, freeing room for amazing opportunities to arrive.

This is a time of grace and patience with yourself. A time to reflect that you are not "better" than anyone else, yet you are strategic about the exposure you experience.

## LESS OVER MORE: KEY INSIGHTS

- **Loneliness kills:** Poor relationships are as harmful as smoking 15 cigarettes daily—quality connections are literally a matter of life and death.
- **Energy is contagious:** You become the average of your five closest friends—choose people who lift you up, not drag you down.
- **Proximity equals productivity:** Being within 25 feet of productive people increases your productivity by 15%; unproductive people decrease it by 30%.
- **Digital detox required:** Limit social media to five check-ins daily—real relationships happen face-to-face, not through screens.
- **Less friends, more life:** Curating a smaller circle of high-quality relationships creates space for deeper connections and greater opportunities.

# CHAPTER 9

# WHEN IS ENOUGH MONEY ENOUGH?

I'll never forget the moment I realized I couldn't pay both my mortgage and my car payment. Early in my entrepreneurial journey, I sat at my desk staring at two bills, knowing one would be late. The shame was crushing. How had I let this happen? After my initial pity party, I made a decision: never again.

But here's what's interesting—that moment of scarcity never truly left me. Even years later, with healthy reserves and consistent income, the old fear would resurface at the slightest business lull. That ancient worry would catapult me into action, pushing me to chase more, more, more—even when I had enough. I was making decisions from scarcity disguised as ambition, taking on clients and projects I should have declined, all because of a fear that no longer matched my reality.

This realization changed everything: I wasn't chasing abundance. I was running from an old wound.

## THE ILLUSION OF "MORE MONEY"

Society teaches us that more money is better—that it's the ultimate symbol of success. Without a clear definition of what "enough" means to you, you'll spend your entire life chasing a moving target that's always just out of reach.

I remember thinking that making $100,000 a year was the pinnacle of success. I firmly believed that when I hit that point, I'd be "rich" and living the life. The truth? I was outspending what I made because I needed the external world to see my wealth through cars, clothes, and experiences. Soon, $100,000 wasn't enough, so the quest for more continued.

I never took note that only 18% of American individuals earn at least $100,000 a year.[28] According to US Census Bureau data, back in the 1990s when I achieved this goal, less than about 4% of the US population earned that much. I was already well within the high-income bracket, yet it never felt like enough. I wonder what would have changed had I known this information versus becoming obsessed with more. Would it have mattered to have known that I was in the top earners?

My quest to make more was endless because I never set a ceiling for what would be enough. The goal—more like a compulsion—was simply more, more, more. It didn't matter how much I was making—it was never really enough. I always craved more, believing that when I made more, I'd finally arrive and be happy and joyful.

Regardless of my income level, the truth was devastating: I arrived at each new peak as the same person with the same issues. In fact, at several income increments, my problems grew because I had to learn how to manage larger quantities of money without understanding what I was really pursuing.

Here's the question that stopped me in my tracks: If my income increased today by tenfold, would my world and the impact I could make actually change? Or would you still feel like you need to make more? Stop and ask yourself that same question—would you feel the need to earn more? I think if we are honest with ourselves, we'd understand that such an increase might calm your desire for more at first . . . yet, in a short amount of time, the need to earn more would emerge—*if* you had no definition of enough.

## WHAT ARE YOU REALLY COLLECTING?

At 18 years old, I discovered credit cards and thought I'd found magic. My parents, children of the Depression, had taught me to buy only what was necessary—no luxuries, no brand names unless they offered better quality, and only paying cash for things. But I wanted to be someone who could buy the brand name just because. I wanted what others with perceived wealth were buying.

My closet looked great. My swagger improved. My confidence walking into rooms went up—until I opened my first month's credit card statement and saw the true cost of "more": the interest charges. I remember thinking, *They were right. These jeans aren't worth it. I had jeans that looked good. This is just a label.*

I wish I could say I only fell into credit card debt once, but I repeated this behavior several times before the lesson truly stuck: Accumulating "more" for the sake of image or having more was not the answer. This pattern revealed a deeper question: Was I collecting money or collecting meaning?

I see people collect money for the sake of having it stashed away, then do nothing but admire their bank balances. They love seeing it grow and knowing they have resources available. But money for the sake of collecting serves no one. Unleveraged money sitting idle has the least true value—it's not creating any meaning beyond the person stashing it away.

Then I heard a leader I respected say, "It isn't about the money. It's about what the money can do." That statement struck me. For the first time, I thought about the responsibility I had to use money to make a difference—to do something full of meaning and see what money could really do.

Yes, I made donations and supported causes near and dear to me. But if I'm completely honest, most of what I did with money was spend it on myself or stash it away to spend on something bigger for myself. It wasn't until I understood "what the money can do" that I realized I had a real responsibility to give my money meaning.

## THE TRUE COST OF "MORE MONEY"

The drive for more comes with a tremendous cost: your time, energy, and presence. These are your most precious assets—things you can't buy and can only experience. Once spent, they're gone forever.

There was a time in my career in the hospitality industry when I took a position requiring extensive travel—sometimes three different cities in one week, other times being away for more than 10 days straight. I was in a relationship at the time, and the job was taking a toll on it.

I'd come home on Friday afternoons wanting nothing more than to sit in my house, absorb the energy of my own space, and recharge. My partner had been home alone all week and wanted to get out—go to dinner, connect with friends. That was the last thing I wanted to do: have another meal out, carrying on conversations with another group of people, when my batteries were completely drained.

In my mind, I was doing this to make more money for us to have a better life. In reality, I was doing the opposite. Not only did my relationship suffer and eventually end, but my health was suffering too. Traveling 80% of the time destroyed my eating habits and workout routines. The "cost" of making more money was substantial, yet I was so caught up in the pursuit that I didn't see it unfolding. Gradually and suddenly, the most important things were collapsing. I had blinders on and could only see more money.

What about the cost to your peace and joy? I watched mine evaporate while chasing numbers that would never be enough.

There were moments when my drive for money took me from my true goals entirely. I took promotions and made career pivots that weren't aligned with my passions—why? Because of the opportunity to make more money.

For instance, I truly loved being in sales in the hospitality industry. I can remember my first real sales job when I moved to Dallas. I could barely wait for my first day. I walked up to the hotel entrance, and the moment I went in, I felt the property's energy and buzz. I quickly introduced myself to the front desk staff, then made my way to the sales offices. I could feel my heart beating in my chest. It was finally here; the day I started my sales career. I truly had found my passion!

At first, I looked forward to each new day and its opportunities. Then my old friend "more" crept in. I noticed the other side of the hospitality industry, operations and all the financial opportunities it brought with it. Ego and money became a driving force. Then I realized that I could become a general manager of my own hotel and it was *game on*! I ended up growing my career in a direction that wasn't my true goal. I lost sight of my real vision and set my sights on bigger paychecks, selling my happiness and true passions for more money.

While I had "more," I ended up with less—the wrong type of less. I was less content, less congruent, less happy, less excited about what I was doing. You see, my true passion for hotel sales was not being met. Even though I excelled in operations, the spark was gone. Promotions continued to follow and took me even further down a path I didn't desire, all for more money.

Has your drive for money taken you from your true goals? Are you doing whatever it takes to get more instead of following your passion? Has your true passion been extinguished in the process?

## ABUNDANCE VERSUS ACCUMULATION

An abundant mindset and a mindset of accumulation can deliver the same financial results, yet one is in alignment with your core beliefs and values, and one is not.

When operating from an abundant mindset, you're in "flow." You're clear in your direction and congruent with your core values. Your thoughts empower you, and your actions and decisions come from your soul, your inner self—fulfilling your passion and dreams. When you're in alignment, amazing things happen. Money flows easily and effortlessly to you. You become a money magnet.

The opposite, the accumulation mindset, is driven by scarcity and evolves from the feeling of fear. Here's how it works: Thoughts create feelings, energy, and emotions, which affect actions and determine your results. If your thoughts of scarcity create feelings of fear, they affect how you act or if you take action at all. Your energy around taking action will be off-putting. You may feel trapped in a downward spiral, a feeling that you have lost control and there is nothing you can do to turn things around. You will continue to be driven by the thoughts of scarcity, a feeling of desperation versus authenticity . . . further driving you away from your goals.

Can you tell the difference when you decide from a place of scarcity versus abundance? Scarcity is just a thought, and you can change it. Thoughts drive all results.

Knowing that this feeling and old way of thinking can be with you for life, is there a way out? Can you create a way to avoid the trap of scarcity? Yes, by creating true freedoms.

## THE THREE FREEDOMS: DEFINING YOUR "ENOUGH"

Here's what changed everything for me: discovering that "enough" wasn't measured by the balance in my bank account, but by the freedoms I'd achieved. Three freedoms define true wealth, and once you understand them, you can finally answer the question: "When is enough money enough?"

### *Financial Freedom: Do What You Want, When You Want, with Whom You Want*

This is the freedom everyone chases but few properly define. Financial freedom means removing all restraints on how you spend your time and with whom you spend it.

One of my favorite leaders from a previous brokerage takes her "girl group" on an annual vacation where she pays for everything. She gets to do what she loves, when she wants, and with whom she wants because she's removed all financial restraints. That's not just wealth—that's freedom.

What does financial freedom look like for you? Not in dollars, but in experiences, choices, and the ability to say yes to what matters without checking your bank account first.

Much like my favorite leader, I love creating experiences for people. Nothing brings me greater joy than creating an experience for someone who might not have the financial resources to do so. To watch their reaction and see the joy is far beyond any financial reward I experience. For me, having the right people on the journey with me is critical. I never want money to be the reason someone important to me can't participate or join me. I love living a big life, and doing it with others is important.

### *Business Freedom: Work Because You Want To, Not Because You Have To*

Imagine working because you love it, not because you need the paycheck. You show up differently when you're focused on the work itself versus the payout. Your creativity flows. Your passion is evident. Your impact multiplies because you're no longer performing for money—you're creating from purpose.

Business freedom doesn't necessarily mean retirement. It means having the choice. Some of the most fulfilled people I know work incredibly hard, but they'd do it even if they weren't paid because it feeds their soul.

### *Spirit Freedom: Create Joy from Within*

This is the freedom most people overlook entirely. Joy is internal—it's not created by an event or external circumstance. Happiness is fleeting, dependent on what's happening around you. Joy comes from within, has staying power, and can be called upon at any time.

Spirit freedom means your sense of peace, fulfillment, and purpose isn't dependent on your bank balance, your title, or what others think of you. It's the ultimate freedom because once it's achieved, nothing external can take it away.

When you define "enough" through these three freedoms rather than a dollar amount, everything changes. Suddenly you're not chasing more money—you're building toward something meaningful. You know when you've arrived because you can feel it in how you live each day.

## FROM ACCUMULATION TO IMPACT: MONEY WITH MEANING

Once I understood the three freedoms, I needed to answer another critical question: How am I making a difference?

Prior to this, I was only asking myself, "How can I make more money?" Without knowing the difference I was making in the world, making money was just a trap—a never-ending pursuit to fill a void instead of my soul.

Once I changed the measuring stick from account balances to the impact I was creating, the fulfillment I was experiencing, and the legacy I was building, money began to have real purpose. Purpose fuels prosperity. When you align your income with impact, wealth becomes more than a number—it becomes a tool for change.

## THE GIFT OF GIVING

Many have echoed the anonymous wisdom that "you have not lived today until you have done something for someone who can never repay you." I've personally found that giving is one of the greatest acts we can do as humans. It's one of the many ways I feel whole and complete when I do something for someone else or an organization.

The amount doesn't matter as much as the willingness to help or contribute to making something or someone better with no expectation of anything in return. If you're operating from scarcity or a "more for me" mentality, giving can seem out of sync. Yet giving at all levels is what can bring you more.

Some may view giving as a "less" move—taking money or time and giving it away, therefore leaving you with less. However, as in all other areas of business and life, this creates space for more to show up. The "more" in this instance may be a feeling: joy, peace, excitement, gratitude. For me, when my bucket gets filled from giving, it's like nothing else I experience.

I regularly support several charities that mean something to me. I may not donate as much as others, but I do what feels right for me. Sometimes I donate time over money, which can have an equal impact. In fact, one of our core values at reTHINK Coaching is that every coach carry one "gratis" client at all times. It's our way of giving back.

The act of giving has the same energetic impact on me as gratitude. It releases all those feel-good dopamine hormones and instantly changes my disposition.

## THE ABUNDANCE PARADOX: HOW LESS FOCUS ON MONEY BRINGS MORE

Here's the paradox I discovered: When you gain clarity around the "why" of your earnings and eliminate the noise of "just make more," you typically end up making more. Like everything else, you start to eliminate the unnecessary and create space for different opportunities to show up.

I learned this lesson in a big way living in Santa Fe, New Mexico. We're a small town of approximately 90,000 people, yet we have over 200 charities that we support as a community. I recently became involved with a few organizations near and dear to my heart.

Placing my money with these organizations and attending their events gave my money meaning. I could watch the difference my gifts made and experience true fulfillment in donating. By participating in these events, I met amazing people—people with whom I had a common bond and automatic connection.

Going to the events, my intention was to have fun, donate, and make a difference. What actually happened? I met incredible people, and through those meetings, opportunities organically appeared: business opportunities that allow me to earn more while doing it in a way that lends to my "spirit freedom."

Focusing less on earning isn't about not making money or stopping your work. It's about aligning your core values and beliefs around money with the impact it can make. Give your money meaning, eliminate the noise of doing more for the sake of doing more, and watch what heads your way.

## WHO DEFINES YOUR ENOUGH?

If you don't define your "enough," someone else will. Usually, it's an employer who benefits from your lack of knowing your enough, ultimately creating burnout and resentment while you build their business, not yours.

Without your definition of enough—like any other goal—you won't know how to get there or what it truly looks like. Then you risk spending your entire life chasing someone else's version of success.

## MAKING YOUR "WHAT IF" INTO "WHAT IS"

One of the most empowering shifts I've made is changing my relationship with money from "what if" to "what is." What if I had more money? What if I could finally afford that? What if I reach that income level?

These "what if" questions keep you perpetually chasing without ever arriving. But when you define your three freedoms—financial, business, and spirit—you shift to "what is." What is my enough? What is my purpose? What is the impact I'm making? What is the legacy I'm building?

True abundance comes when you stop the noise and start tuning into your mental, emotional, and spiritual needs. Being fulfilled is not a byproduct of wealth—it's a prerequisite for meaningful success. Choose to build a legacy that speaks louder than your lifestyle.

Because at the end of it all, money without meaning is meaningless.

## THE PATH FORWARD

Like other areas of "more," money can become part of your endless pursuit. But what if we redirected the "more" drive and replaced it with meaning? Could you reach an impactful meaning while doing "less"? Absolutely.

Many people believe money gives them meaning, but in truth, *you* give *money* meaning. The shift happens when you:

1. **define your three freedoms** with specific clarity;
2. **calculate your actual "enough" number** based on those freedoms, not arbitrary comparisons;
3. **align your income with impact** by giving your money purpose;
4. **operate from abundance,** not scarcity, recognizing when fear is driving decisions; and
5. **create space through giving,** knowing that what you release creates room for what you need.

When you become intentional about these elements, you stop chasing more and start building meaning. Your journey to "enough" is uniquely yours. It won't look like anyone else's, and that's exactly as it should be. The question isn't how much money you need to be happy—it's what freedoms you're building toward and what impact you're making along the way.

Because true wealth isn't measured by what you accumulate. It's measured by the life you live, the difference you make, and the freedom you've created to be fully yourself.

That's when enough becomes more than enough. That's when you discover that less focus on money creates space for more life, more joy, more purpose, more impact, and ironically, more prosperity than you ever imagined.

What if we reframed "When is enough, enough?" to "*When does enough signal it's time to give back?*" If you have never given for the sake of giving with no expectation in return, I can't recommend it enough. It doesn't have to be big; it can be simple. Maybe paying for the person's coffee in the line behind you. Giving the cashier a $100 bill and telling them to use it for those in line with *no* mention of who gave the $100. Much like wringing out the sponge for opportunity, we can wring out the sponge of money and create the space for more to come.

## LESS OVER MORE: KEY INSIGHTS

- **Define your three freedoms:** Financial (do what you want, when, with whom), Business (work because you want to, not have to), and Spirit (create joy from within)—these are the real measures of wealth.
- **Scarcity repels; abundance attracts:** Money decisions driven by fear push opportunities away; decisions from alignment draw prosperity effortlessly.
- **Without defining "enough," you chase forever:** If you don't determine your own "enough," you'll spend your life pursuing someone else's moving target while building their dreams.
- **Money without meaning is meaningless:** True fulfillment comes from aligning income with impact, giving your money purpose beyond accumulation.
- **Giving creates space for receiving:** Whether money or time, what you release creates room for more to flow into your life—less focus on getting more actually brings more.

# PART IV

# ABUNDANCE THROUGH LESS

CHAPTER 10

# WHAT TO DO WITH YOUR OLD THOUGHTS

Earlier in my life, the thought that kept running its course through my mind was one of scarcity: save your money, only buy what's necessary, keep things until they no longer work. This programming was embedded by my parents, and I absorbed their ideology completely.

My dad had a particular way of making you question every purchase: "Gosh, I hope you like that. You know that money is now gone and you can't get it back." "Did you really need that?" "What else could you have used that money on?" "What if you need that money in the future and it's gone?" I know this came from a place of concern, but he really made it difficult to enjoy purchasing nearly anything, almost removing my joy before I even paid for the item. I still occasionally find myself looking for the "return policy" on purchases. Reading contracts looking for the "out." Still hearing my dad's voice and seeking an escape clause if I ever have buyer's remorse or feel that the purchase was frivolous.

When I entered the workforce and started earning my own real money, seeing how others lived triggered my "more" existence. Yet as much as I started to spend, gather, and accumulate, the old thought kept playing in my head. It felt like buyer's remorse, but it ran deeper—a sense of irresponsibility that triggered "more." More served as my medication against the scarcity mindset, numbing me just long enough to buy more . . . then the old thoughts would come racing back. It was a vicious cycle, and I did my best to push those thoughts down, to ignore them or pretend they didn't exist.

Yet this I know to be true: When you resist or "push" things down, it is like holding a beach ball under water. You can only do it for so long before the ball comes flying out of the water, usually smacking you in the face. As hard as I tried to push the thoughts down, they would emerge!

Those thoughts were definitely running a program in the background, surfacing more often than I care to admit.

So, here's the million-dollar question: Do old thoughts truly die?

## WHERE OLD THOUGHTS GO: NOT DEATH, BUT TRANSFORMATION

Old thoughts don't die. They just get quieter and visit less often. They're with us for life, yet we can have more control over them. We can become aware of their presence quicker and can reframe them to actually support us instead of hindering us.

I will never forget sitting in a coaches' training session when the facilitator said, "You know, your old thoughts are with you to the grave! It is up to you to manage them, yet know they will be with you and emerge in times of uncertainty or stress." *What*, you mean I have done all this work only to have them not go away? *Yes!* However, knowledge is power, and the simple awareness of that allowed me to look at those old disempowering thoughts differently.

When I learned and became certified in NLP, I discovered that these disempowering thoughts were part of the 80% of negative thoughts we have every day. Remember, we have an average of 60,000 thoughts daily, 80% negative, 95% repetitive. I also learned that despite our advancement as a species, our brains still have very primitive elements. They process change and uncertainty as "danger"—much like back in cave-dwelling days when you'd have to forage for food and hope you didn't get killed.

When the brain sees something as dangerous, it can flood your mind with negative thoughts and prevent you from taking action. So, when I wanted to eliminate scarcity thinking, my brain initially viewed it as "danger" and did its best to keep me in that familiar space, because it didn't know how to handle the shift to abundant thinking. It flooded my mind with thoughts that tossed me into a scarcity mindset, convincing me to "play it safe."

## THE NEURAL HIGHWAY SYSTEM

Every time we have a thought, neurons fire impulses that travel down a neural pathway to extract information about what to do with that thought—actually, what to think about the thought and give it meaning. Your brain is full of neural pathways that operate much like a highway system. Year after year, the same thoughts carve deep pathways into your mind, much as a river flowing over rock cuts deeper channels over time.

When you begin using the tools I've introduced—specifically the Thought Flow Model—you're creating a new pathway, one that hasn't been traveled much by your brain and it will feel different. Think about driving familiar highways to a place you visit often. Suddenly, one day a detour sign forces you in a different direction.

At first, having to pay more attention may feel confusing. Yet, if this detour remains for months, it becomes more familiar, much as your old route was. Then one day, the detour sign is gone, and you get to decide, "Do I go back to the old route or continue on the new path that's been created?" The old route doesn't go away—it's always an option—and after traveling the new route, it may not feel as comfortable as the detour.

Likewise, your old thoughts are no longer true—they're just familiar. You'll notice over time that you have them less often and will begin to release them. There will be moments when they appear, especially during times of stress, anxiety, fear, or even joy. But the quicker you realize they're not your truth any longer, the quicker you can choose the right pathway.

How did I retrain my brain? How did I get my scarcity thinking to quiet down? I spent considerable time exploring what I was making scarcity mean. What story was I holding onto about it? What feelings were present when I was in that state of mind? What did it do to my ability to take action or move forward? Ultimately, what was the impact on my life and results? I firmly believe releasing these thoughts was the catalyst for my "less" life. Once I was able to reframe these thoughts, give them new meaning, and use them to my advantage, I started to slow down on the consumption and gathering activities. It was the beginning of a peaceful and joy-filled existence.

## HONORING THE SURVIVAL MECHANISM

The version of you that holds the old thoughts? That version was one of survival. It was how you made it to where you are today, and at one point, it served a purpose. Those thoughts guided you and protected you on your old journey. We must acknowledge their usefulness during that phase.

This awareness became a turning point for me. Initially, I found myself annoyed with the old thought patterns, wanting to disassociate from them as quickly as possible because the new me was bursting at the seams to get out. What I learned was that I had to honor the good in those old thoughts—wisdom. Yes, it seems counterintuitive, and I feel that realizing this was the breaking point that released some of my anger and resentment, allowing me to embrace the new. I took time to extract that wisdom and learn from it. This process released my negative emotions around the old thoughts and gave me a deeper understanding of why they existed in the first place.

My parents' voices around spending money will forever live in my head. I've come to terms with this, and it makes me smile. I know that wherever my parents are now, they see things differently. I always thank them for their concern and reflect on the purpose and joy of the item I am purchasing. If those two elements aren't present with a purchase, I'll say no—a no that comes not from scarcity but from purpose.

## THE WEIGHT OF REGRET: WHEN THE PAST HOLDS THE PEN

I had plenty of regrets about my "more" phase. Those regrets stirred up thoughts that weighed heavily on me—the deals I blew, the opportunities I missed, the people I may have hurt along the way, the lost time with family and friends.

When I left my corporate career to become an entrepreneur, I occasionally allowed myself to live in the space of regret. I created a story in my mind about how wonderful it would have been, how different my life would be if I'd just stayed. The regret of the great perceived missed opportunity would surface primarily when things weren't going well in my real estate career or entrepreneurial growth phases.

One significant event stirred up the greatest space of regret. I'd been a licensed Realtor for just six months when the events of September 11 happened. I had multiple transactions in escrow, and one by one, each person called to cancel their contract at any cost. I went months with no income as the real estate market came to a standstill. I was drowning in regretful thoughts, running scenarios in my mind about what my life would have looked like if I'd just stayed with the hospitality industry.

The reality? That industry was hit just as hard during this time, and there was no guarantee my job would have been secure. Yet my mind created a different version of the truth.

I was fortunate to be working for an amazing broker at the time. One of the senior Realtors clearly saw the turmoil I was in and took me aside to coach me through the moment. She helped me write a different story and change my thoughts about the opportunities that were coming. In that moment, I let go of some of the regret and started reframing the thoughts and stories I was holding onto. In a blink, my business and life changed. One simple yet powerful conversation with a caring peer changed everything.

## UNDERSTANDING REGRET'S POWER

Regret is a significant driver in our thoughts and one of the key issues we must address. Think back to the Thought Flow Model: Something happens → Thoughts → Feelings/Energy/Emotion → Actions → Results. Regret is a "something that happens" that creates a cascade of disempowering thoughts.

For instance: "I regret not taking that next step in my career before I quit" creates the thought, "My life could be so different. I'd have more money, more retirement." That generates feelings of frustration and sadness, energy that's nonexistent. Actions become "Why bother? I can never achieve what I could have had," leading to results of limited success and a growth ceiling.

Research from Cornell University found that people regret actions more in the short term ("I shouldn't have said that") but regret inaction in the long term ("I wish I would have done X").[29] Inaction regrets linger much longer because they leave open possibilities—the lack of closure means the "what ifs" can be endless.

Here's the empowering truth: Regret is universal, and you get to determine whether it's a negative force or a powerful tool for growth.

## TRANSFORMING REGRET INTO WISDOM

When regret visits, I've learned to ask it what it's teaching me. What was driving the decision I made? When I remove the emotion and look for facts, I often find positive elements in that decision worth acknowledging.

If regret lingers, it's often because it's unresolved. Sometimes you need closure—to send the message you never sent, even if you write a letter and never mail it. Share your truth transparently. Do what you wanted to do but resisted—take that course, pursue that hobby, make that leap.

I also revisit the event causing regret and show myself grace. I accept that I made the decision with the knowledge I had at the time. Is it possible that if I'd made the alternate choice, I wouldn't have the opportunities I now have? Almost certainly.

What "should have, could have, would have" are you holding onto? When I hear someone use those words, I know they're living in the space of regret. Those phrases signal that it's time to rewrite the story and put closure on what no longer supports you or moves you forward.

## THE VOICE IN YOUR HEAD: MANAGING SELF-TALK

Have you ever stopped to listen to the conversations you have with yourself? We can be the person who's the most cruel and demeaning to ourselves. The self-talk we engage in influences the bits of data we collect throughout the day and begins creating a case for our results. The inner critic that resides in you—fueled by you—can be the loudest voice you hear, influencing your thoughts and behaviors.

The voice in your head is not you. It's a default mechanism you've used for years, judging yourself more harshly than others would judge you. It sounds like: "I'm such an idiot." "I always mess up." "I can't believe I was that stupid." "Why can't I do anything right?" These statements are not true. Are you an idiot? Do you always mess up? Are you truly stupid? Do you not do anything right?

I learned to distance myself from these thoughts by naming the voice. "Ah, there's thoughtless Tony again with his nonsense, speaking nontruths and trying to make me feel bad." Giving the voice a separate identity helps you recognize it's not your true self speaking—it's just old programming.

## INTERRUPTING THE PATTERN

The moment you catch the negative commentary, interrupt it quickly. Use Byron Katie's Four Questions, starting with, "Is this thought true?" When you flip the script from "I always mess up" to "When I make mistakes, I'm taking action and learning things that work and don't work—I'm growing," you create a new pathway.

But awareness and interruption alone aren't enough. You must feed the voice and thoughts you want to grow.

There's a parable often ascribed to Cherokee folklore about an elder brave telling his grandson about a battle that goes on inside people. "My son, the battle is between two wolves inside us all. One is evil—it is anger, envy, jealousy, sorrow, regret, greed, arrogance, self-pity, guilt, resentment, inferiority, lies, false pride, superiority, and ego. The other is good—it is joy, peace, love, hope, serenity, humility, kindness, benevolence, empathy, generosity, truth, compassion, and faith."

The grandson asks, "Which wolf wins?"

The elder replies, "The one you feed."

You get to decide which voice or thought you will feed and nurture, which will grow inside you and write your story. How do you feed the one you want?

## THE POWER OF "I AM"

Whatever you say after "I am" is what you will become. These statements speak directly to your identity, tapping into your deepest level of belief about yourself. They create new neural pathways, and when you say them repeatedly, they become a new highway for your mind to use.

"I am" statements activate your brain to focus on the greatness you're claiming. What you focus on expands, and your brain goes to work finding evidence of this truth throughout your day. They rewire self-talk and plant the belief in the present moment, not some far-off unknown timeline.

Your unconscious mind can't tell the difference between reality and make-believe—it takes what you tell it as truth. But "I am" statements only work when repeated frequently and when you have some level of belief in them. There must be a sense of reality connected to them.

For example, if you currently have $10,000 in savings and earn $70,000 per year, stating "I am a millionaire" likely won't work because there's a significant gap between reality and the desired state. Use bridging statements instead: "I am becoming a millionaire" or "I am building wealth every day."

## THE TRANSFORMATION TOOLKIT: DAILY PRACTICES THAT REWIRE YOUR BRAIN

Awareness is powerful, but transformation requires action. I discovered three practices that fundamentally changed how I relate to my thoughts: journaling, meditation, and consistent application through what I call the 30-Day Thought Sprint.

### *Journaling: The Thought Laboratory*

I remember countless failed attempts at journaling—the new journals I'd buy, believing "this one will be different." Yet time and again, I'd sit with a blank page taunting me. "What do you say? What are you going to write? This is stupid. What if someone reads your thoughts?" I had story after story about why journaling wasn't for me, and guess what? It wasn't—until I decided to get serious about my thought work.

I dug out one of the many empty journals and started writing with an outline that helped me process my thoughts in a structured way. Each morning, I'd explore what was on my mind, what I was feeling and why, what I wanted to focus on and potentially change, what new thought I'd like to choose, and what action would make the greatest impact.

The key breakthrough came when I tied journaling to something I already loved: coffee. I set a rule that I could only have my first cup while sitting and journaling. If I didn't journal, no coffee. This pushed me into the activity, and before long, it no longer felt like a chore. It became a place where I could work out my thoughts, reflect, and create an amazing future, because my thoughts were in alignment with my success.

## *Meditation: Quieting the Noise*

I resisted meditation for years. I couldn't grasp sitting in silence with my thoughts. I found myself thinking about everything but my thoughts: "What's for dinner tonight? I forgot to send that email. What's the weather going to be like?" I was masterful at distracting myself.

My coach recommended guided meditations to help me stay focused and flow into the practice more easily. Meditation helped me remove the noise and calm my brain, getting to the space of focusing on the thoughts I wanted to infuse into my day and life. If I ever miss a day of either journaling or meditating, I can feel the difference. I'm "off" for the entire day. Something is missing, and I go into the day with less clarity and focus. I have more doubts, and old thoughts return more easily. Journaling and meditation have become my way to tame the "beast" of my old thoughts while being purposeful and honest.

## *The 30-Day Thought Sprint: Your Transformation Blueprint*

Changing and redirecting your thoughts is a tremendous opportunity, but it's not accomplished by dabbling in the process. Like everything else, consistency is the key that separates those who succeed from those who think it's a great idea to succeed.

For me, consistency was the missing element for longer than I care to admit. I'd journal and work on my thoughts, but as soon as the journal closed for the day, it was as if I became a different person. It was easy to "say it, think it, and write it," but not so easy to "be it" and "do it."

This sequence—often summarized as "Be, then Do, then Have"—emerges from identity-based change work found in neuro-linguistic programming and was popularized in leadership literature through Stephen Covey's inside-out philosophy:

- **BE:** This is who you must "be" to achieve your goals—your identity, character, and mindset. It's about cultivating the qualities and beliefs that align with your desired outcome.
- **DO:** This is the action and behavior part that must be consistent with the desired identity and outcome—the part many of us resist.
- **HAVE:** This is where your desired results and achievements happen due to who you decided to "be" and what you decided to "do."

I loved living in the "have"—it felt so good to "have" more powerful thoughts, fewer negative thoughts, and amazing results. But the "be" and the "do" were weak and not in alignment with my "have." That changed when I challenged myself to a 30-day sprint. I knew it would take a process and a path, not just hope and prayer.

## THE SPRINT PROCESS: STEP BY STEP

Here's exactly what I did, and what transformed my relationship with my thoughts:

**Each Morning:** Along with my standard journal practice, I implemented a "thought dump" exercise and bought another journal exclusively for this. For 10 minutes, I stayed in a state of flow and dumped all my thoughts on paper without lifting my pen until the timer went off. I wrote down every single thought I was having and resisted the urge to justify or solve any thought. The first day I did this, I was mortified to realize that I wasn't special—80% of my thoughts were negative, just like the research says.

**Assessment:** I'd review the thoughts and pick out the top negative thought—the biggest gut punch that hit me the hardest. I picked it on instinct as I sorted through everything, without overanalyzing. That's how I knew which one needed to be addressed.

**Unconscious Thought Flow:** I took that negative thought and ran it through the Thought Flow Model, seeing the impact it had on my feelings, energy, emotions, potential actions, and forecasted results. I labeled this my "unconscious thought flow model."

**Reframing:** Next, I ran the thought through Byron Katie's Four Questions to reframe it from a negative thought to an empowering one.

**Conscious Thought Flow:** I took the new version of the thought—the empowering one—and ran it through the Thought Flow Model to see the difference. I could see the impact on feelings, energy, emotions, actions, and forecasted results. I called this my "conscious thought flow model" because I'd now made it a conscious thought.

**Future Pacing:** I took the results line from the model and treated it as if it already happened. I'd write a paragraph as if the result had already occurred: "Today was an amazing day. I focused on [empowering thought], and amazing things happened. I connected with my clients and had great conversations. In fact, a client that I have been working with for nearly one year agreed to work with me. I have appointments set for next week . . ."

**Daily Reminder:** I made a note in my phone with the new thought written out and kept it with me all day. Even though I spent considerable time on the thought process in the morning, the old thought would creep in throughout the day. Having the reframed thought with me helped me quiet the old thought quicker. I'd also keep the future-pacing paragraph and read it when the old thought became noisy.

**Commitment:** I did this exercise for 30 days, accepting that 80% of my thoughts would be negative each day and 95% were familiar because they were repetitive. I realized I was pulling unconscious thoughts that were harming my life and business into my conscious awareness. Once I had them in my conscious sight, I could do something about them.

## THE RESULTS: LIVING IN FLOW

The end result? I was able to spend more time in the 20% positive category and had the new thought with me because it now lived in that space. To say the results were impressive is an understatement. I entered what I call "the flow state"—that state of mind and being when things fall into place and seem to happen like magic. Things I didn't expect showed up, and "more" of what I desired began to happen.

The 30-Day Thought Sprint became the bridge between my old way of thinking and my new potential. It wasn't magic. It was consistency, intention, and the willingness to sit with uncomfortable truths long enough to transform them.

## WHO HOLDS THE PEN?

Rewriting your story with new, empowering thoughts is one of the best gifts you can give yourself. Your story is always being written. The question is, who's holding the pen? My hope is that it's you picking up the pen and writing your future, your desires, and your dreams. Where will your old thoughts go? If you aren't purposeful, they'll remain front and center, wielding the pen that writes your future.

The journey from old thoughts to new ones isn't about perfection. It's about progress. Some days you'll catch the old thoughts quickly and redirect them effortlessly. Other days, you'll realize hours later that you've been running old programs. That's okay. The neural pathways you're building get stronger every time you choose the new route, even when you occasionally default to the old one.

Remember, your old thoughts served a purpose. They kept you safe, helped you survive, and got you to where you are today. Honor them for that. Thank them for their service. And then gently, consistently, choose the new pathway that leads to the life you're creating now.

The transformation isn't instant, but it is inevitable when you commit to the process. Every morning you journal, every moment you interrupt negative self-talk, every time you choose the empowering thought over the familiar one, you're building new neural highways. You're feeding the wolf you want to win.

Your new potential isn't waiting for perfect conditions or complete transformation. It's available right now, at this moment, with the next thought you choose. The old thoughts will visit—let them. Acknowledge them, thank them for their concern, and then choose differently.

## LESS OVER MORE: KEY INSIGHTS

- **Old thoughts don't die, they transform:** Your disempowering thoughts will visit less often as you build new neural pathways—they're not your enemy, they're old survival mechanisms that need honoring before releasing.
- **Regret is a teacher, not a life sentence:** Use the Thought Flow Model to transform regret from a circumstance that creates disempowerment into wisdom that propels you forward.
- **Feed the wolf you want to win:** Self-talk shapes reality—name your inner critic, interrupt negative patterns quickly, and use "I am" statements to create your new identity.
- **Consistency beats intensity:** The 30-Day Thought Sprint works because daily practice builds neural highways—transformation comes from showing up every day, not from perfect execution.
- **You hold the pen:** You are writing your story right now—choose whether old thoughts or new potential will write your future through intentional daily practices of journaling, meditation, and thought reframing.

# CHAPTER 11

# THE LESS AND MORE OF HEALTH

Of all the areas where *more* can have a negative impact, health might be the most important. We chase more workouts, more supplements, more diets, more tracking, more intensity—believing that more effort equals more health. We turn wellness into warfare, treating our bodies like machines that need constant upgrading rather than humans who need sustainable care.

But what if the opposite is true? What if the path to genuine health isn't found in adding more but in releasing the excess that's exhausting us?

Without your health, nothing else matters. You can have clarity on your Why, amazing relationships, and financial freedom, but if your body breaks down from the *more* you've demanded of it, none of those other victories count for much.

## THE WAKE-UP CALL I NEVER SAW COMING

The importance of my health was never more evident than in 2016. I got married that year, and like many significant life events, I wanted to enter it in the best shape of my life. Out of the blue—what I later understood as a God thing—I decided to start running. At 40-something years of age, I'd never run a day in my life. As a kid with asthma, running wasn't even on the radar. Yet suddenly, I started. It was a gradual process, yet, I found myself running five miles a day, feeling strong, feeling invincible. Then everything changed.

Upon returning from an international trip in the fall of 2016, I started feeling off. I couldn't catch my stride. Running became challenging, and I developed a weird cough. My physician diagnosed allergies. I started allergy medication, but the cough grew worse. I went from running five miles a day to being unable to walk from my car into the grocery store without stopping multiple times to catch my breath.

Several visits to my physician ensued, but we found no answers or cures for what was happening, and my condition grew worse. My last visit was January 6, 2017—five months after my first symptoms—when he advised it must be mental and prescribed Xanax. I told him what he could do with his prescription and left.

On Monday, January 9, I woke up worse than ever. I remember having to sit on the ground to brush my teeth because I couldn't stand without nearly passing out. I thought, *Maybe it really is allergies, and I just haven't treated them properly.* I found an allergist who could see me *that* day (another God moment). My sister, a nurse, hopped on a call with me during my exam with the allergist. The allergist stated that I might have a lung infection or lung cancer but not allergies. My sister, being persistent, convinced her to order a scan of my lungs.

When the scan was complete, the technician's face told me everything. "Don't move," she kept saying. "Don't tap a finger, a toe. Lay perfectly still."

The doctor came in and delivered the news: My lungs were full of blood clots—pulmonary embolisms. I needed to get to the hospital immediately.

I was admitted to the cardiac ICU. Every doctor who saw my scans said the same thing: "You're a miracle. You dodged a bullet. We only see films like this when we do autopsies." I had dozens of clots, including a saddle embolism—the one you don't want—the one that can have catastrophic results. They recommended a risky procedure because my choices weren't plentiful.

As they prepped me for the procedure, I asked the entire medical team to gather around my table. I told them that anyone who had doubts about a successful outcome should leave the room. I only wanted people who believed in a positive result. We agreed on '80s music in the room (though some of the younger staff probably thought I'd chosen an oldies station). The sedation didn't work—I was alert for the entire procedure, feeling them enter my neck and work into my lungs.

I survived. Many don't—I'm one of the lucky ones. My cardiologist firmly believes a major component of my survival was my heart and lung health going into the event—health I'd built through running.

## THE FORCED RESET: WHEN LESS BECOMES MANDATORY

This event put my health in a situation I'd never experienced before. My old routine—weight training, cardio twice a day, and a mountain of supplements—had to stop. I was restricted to minimal activity, and doctors told me to immediately quit the supplements, especially fat burners, which were affecting my heart. My health regime as I knew it was done.

The break from my fitness routine forced me to focus on "less"—and I mean, you can't do much less than nothing. My body was in total recovery mode, specifically my heart and lungs. My only instructions were to listen to my body and ease back in.

But this forced stillness allowed for something unexpected: space for new things to enter my fitness world. We'd just relocated to California and joined a club with an amazing spa and workout facility. Initially, I started following old patterns of "more"—elliptical, StairMaster, rowing machine—filling the space with activities. I was quickly reminded that my body would resist these old activities, and I found myself lost and miserable.

My coach encouraged me to get clear on what my true goal was. I'd lost my identity as a runner. The wedding was behind us. I hadn't cleared space for a new goal, and to me, healthy meant running. Without that activity, I risked falling back to "unhealthy."

Once I redefined my goals and gave them different meanings, things changed. Rather than jumping into the deep end, I committed to taking on one new activity at a time—not overwhelming my brain with too much, staying focused on my big goal of rebuilding my lungs and getting my heart healthy again.

I also surrendered obsessing over every bit of food, every calorie, every workout. This kept me out of overwhelm. Real freedom comes when we let go of obsessions. What showed up for me was space for true nourishment and movement that actually felt good, both physically and spiritually. Joy doesn't come from extremes—it comes from balance.

## THE NOISE WE CARRY: MY RESISTANCE TO SILENCE

On my health recovery journey, I experienced tremendous noise—in the form of disempowering thoughts. I resisted downtime because it only fueled negative thinking: "What if I never figure this out and get out of shape again? What if I can't regain my lung and heart function? What if this is as good as it gets? What if it happens again?"

The noise was growing, truly deafening.

Here's what you need to know about me: If you'd visited my home before this awakening, music was always playing in the background. Always. I lived in a space of constant noise humming around me. I honestly thought it was good for me, that it created energy and atmosphere. What I didn't realize was that it was just noise keeping me from my inner thoughts and preventing my body from truly resting and recovering.

I was terrified of silence. I believed silence gave my brain permission to run wild, that it would allow the thoughts I was avoiding to emerge and force me to deal with them. The irony isn't lost on me now—someone who preaches that thoughts drive all results was actively avoiding his own thoughts.

It was through work with a coach specializing in mind, body, and spirit that I was introduced to the gift of silence. I quickly learned that silence significantly affects overall health, specifically on the parasympathetic nervous system. This part of your nervous system helps control your body's response during rest—it's your "rest and digest" system that balances out your "fight or flight" response. When I discovered that silence activates this system, allowing your body to truly rest and recover, everything changed.

But if you're anything like me, you rarely have silence as part of your routine or even consider its impact. Truly, who has time for silence when you're living the "more" life? I didn't—until I was forced to.

## THE SCIENCE OF STILLNESS

Once I embraced silence and made it part of my daily routine, I truly understood its power. Like everything else, it took intention and clearing space to allow it room in my life. I leaned into experts and began a meditation practice and breathwork.

What I discovered shocked me. Silence doesn't just feel good—it measurably improves health in profound ways.

A 2005 study shows that just two minutes of silence after listening to music significantly reduces heart rate and blood pressure—even more than slow, relaxing music.[30] For someone recovering from pulmonary embolisms, this wasn't just interesting; it was lifesaving. Chronically noisy environments increase your heart rate and blood pressure, essentially keeping your body in a constant state of low-level stress.

Research also reveals that silence improves concentration and focus. When participants performed tasks requiring concentration with silence, speech, or other noise in the background, those who worked in silence experienced the least cognitive load and lowest stress levels. As psychologist Supriya Blair explains, "Focusing on one thing at a time with one's full attention can help promote efficiency and calmness amid activity. Life happens in order. When we focus on one thing at a time, we are not scattered."[31]

Perhaps most surprisingly, silence can calm racing thoughts—the hallmark of anxiety. When you're focused on "more," it naturally leads to anxiety. I initially believed that silence would give my racing thoughts free rein, that the quiet would become filled with swirling worries. Blair addresses this perfectly: "Learning how to become quiet helps us refrain from expending unnecessary energy, endlessly participating in the hamster wheel of thoughts in our head."

A 2013 study on mice from Duke University[32] found that silence may stimulate brain growth. Animal studies found that two hours of silence stimulated growth of new cells in the hippocampus—the region of the brain related to memory and emotion. While scientists can't guarantee the same happens in humans, it's a compelling possibility.

Silence also reduces cortisol, the stress hormone. The same study that showed noise's effects on concentration found that people who performed tasks with background noise had elevated cortisol levels. As clinical psychologist Martine Prunty explains, "An accumulation of unpleasant noise can lead to mental stress and an excess release of cortisol. When it becomes elevated, it can lead to weight gain, feelings of significant overwhelm, difficulties sleeping, and chronic diseases."[33]

Beyond physical health, silence stimulates creativity. Creating space for silence in your head can be key to increased creativity, as periods of downtime have been found to increase productivity and improve problem-solving skills. It can reduce insomnia—for many, silence and quiet are essential for restful sleep. And perhaps most importantly, silence encourages mindfulness, providing an invitation to sit with the present moment.

What I've learned as I've grown comfortable with silence is that it truly is the greatest move toward "less." Removing external distractions and leaning into silence creates space to receive more—more creativity, more peace, more mindfulness, calmer thoughts, and a quieter mind. Like other areas of "less," it has created space for the right things to show up in my life, business, and relationships.

When was the last time you allowed yourself to sit in total silence? No distractions, no phone buzzing or beeping, no TV, no electronic devices, no scrolling, no background noise—just solitude with you and your thoughts? If you're like most people, the only time you experience silence is when you sleep.

## THE BALANCE TRAP: RESTING VERSUS CHASING

Has your quest for health turned into a grind? Are you racing around in the wee hours of the morning or late hours of the evening to wedge in training or workout programs? Have you created a "more" situation with your health that's actually creating a potential health issue? Are you depriving yourself of rest and recovery time?

We've all met that person who shares their aggressive workout routine—all the time spent at the gym, the multiple programs or classes they attend—and then shares how exhausted they are. My favorite is running into someone at the gym in the early morning hours who talks about how tired they are, how they had to force themselves out of bed, how worn out they are—but how they have so many workout commitments.

I, too, have been caught in the frenzy of multiple workout sessions, pushing myself toward greater health but at the cost of many other things—breaking important boundaries I had with commitments to family and friends.

The time leading up to my wedding is a prime example of not honoring other areas of my life because I was in a "more" phase. I filled my days with training sessions, early-morning runs, and late-evening runs, which created a cascade of "no's" in my life. No, I can't do dinner—I need to go for a run. No, I can't go to happy hour—I need to hit the gym. No, I can't eat that—it's not on my restricted diet plan.

As they say, you can't live in reverse. I can't undo the missed memories; I can only learn from that experience and figure out my path forward.

The wedding prep obsession revealed something critical: I'd turned health into another form of "more"—another area where accumulation and intensity became badges of honor rather than sustainable practices that enhanced my life. I was so focused on looking good in wedding photos that I sacrificed the joy of the journey. I was building a body while depleting my spirit.

The irony is stunning: I was destroying my relationships and peace of mind in pursuit of physical health, not realizing that true health is holistic. You can't compartmentalize wellness. Mental health, emotional health, relational health, and physical health are interconnected. Sacrificing three for one isn't healthy—it's an obsession disguised as discipline.

## FINDING YOUR RHYTHM: WHEN LESS CREATES MORE HEALTH

For me, I've found true balance when it comes to health. I'm one of those people who naturally wake up at 4:30 AM—no alarms needed, it's just the natural rhythm of my body. I found the perfect workout plan that helps with both balance and clarity.

I became a yogi.

If you'd ever told me I'd be all in on the yoga world, I probably would have laughed and said, "Are you kidding? Stretching isn't going to do much for my health." I'd spent decades believing that health required intensity—that if you weren't sweating profusely, gasping for air, and pushing to exhaustion, you weren't really working out.

Fortunately, a friend introduced me to hot yoga, and my life hasn't been the same since. Five to six days a week, you'll find me at the 7 AM Power Flow, Quick and Dirty, or 26:2 Hot Yoga classes. I get my workout in before starting my workday, and it's a solid part of my morning routine. It has helped with mental clarity, focus, and physical strength.

This one thing has worked brilliantly for me, and it's "less" than my old workout routines while providing more health benefits. It has lifted my mental health as well. I set an intention before each session and focus on that for 60 minutes, blocking out the noise of everything else and implementing the discipline to focus and be present.

The beauty of yoga is that it doesn't demand more time, more equipment, more tracking, or more obsession. It's one practice that addresses multiple dimensions of health simultaneously—strength, flexibility, balance, breath, mindfulness, and mental clarity. For me, it's the epitome of Less Over More.

What would be your ideal health routine? What makes you energized and happy, giving you a surge of endorphins to supercharge your day? Also—and this might be more important—what are you doing that's actually hindering your overall health? Have you overcommitted or created an unrealistic schedule?

## HEALTH AS FOUNDATION

Here's what I've learned through nearly dying and then learning to truly live: Health is the crux of all other things. You're not a machine in a warehouse or equipment room that runs independently, needing only an occasional "upgrade" to make it more efficient. You're a human functioning in the world, and everything else in this book—your Why, your values, your relationships, your relationship with money, your thought patterns, all of it—rests on the foundation of your health.

You cannot sustain a "less" life in business if your body is breaking down from the "more" you demand of it. You cannot be present in your relationships if you're exhausted from overtraining or depleted from a restrictive diet. You cannot make clear decisions about your path forward if your cortisol is constantly elevated from lack of rest.

The path to health through "less" isn't about doing nothing—it's about doing what matters with intention and releasing what doesn't serve you. It's about finding your rhythm rather than following someone else's program. It's about balance over intensity, sustainability over extremes, and joy over obsession.

To be clear, I'm not giving medical advice—I recommend consulting with your healthcare professional before implementing any changes. I'm sharing what has worked for me and for those I coach and spend time with.

I will say this: If you're running yourself into the ground in pursuit of health, you've missed the point entirely. True health—the kind that sustains you through decades, not just weeks—comes from less stress, not more; less obsession, not more; less noise, not more; less pushing, not more.

It comes from finding your rhythm and honoring it, even when the world tells you that more is the only way.

## LESS OVER MORE: KEY INSIGHTS

- **Health is the foundation for everything:** Without your health, clarity on your Why, curated relationships, and financial freedom mean nothing—you can't sustain a "less" life while demanding "more" from your body.
- **Silence isn't empty, it's essential:** Two minutes of silence can lower blood pressure more than relaxing music, reduce cortisol, improve focus, and create space for creativity. The noise you carry is likely harming your health.
- **Rest is not weakness, it's wisdom:** True health comes from balance between exertion and recovery—overtraining and obsessive routines create the same exhaustion as "more" in business while sacrificing joy and relationships.
- **One sustainable practice beats multiple fragmented ones:** Finding your rhythm (like yoga replacing multiple workouts) delivers more comprehensive benefits with less time, stress, and complexity than chasing endless programs.
- **Audio must match video:** Track your actual health activities for seven days to see if what you're doing matches what you're saying—awareness of the gap between intention and action is the first step to sustainable change.

CHAPTER 12

# WANT WHAT YOU WANT

What do you want?

This simple question can cause tremendous distress and confusion. I've watched successful people—CEOs, entrepreneurs, high achievers—freeze when asked this question. Their mouths open, then close. They stammer. They deflect. They tell me what they *don't* want instead.

In our quest for more, we often hide what we want and conform to what we're expected to be. After enough time passes, we can't even remember what it is we want. The muscle of desiring has atrophied from decades of disuse. We've become experts at accepting what's given rather than reaching for what calls to us.

But here's what I've discovered after 15-plus years of coaching: Your "don't wants" are actually a treasure map. Every frustration, every complaint, every "I don't want this" is a clue pointing directly to what you do want. You just need to learn how to read the map.

## THE CONDITIONING BEGINS: LEARNING TO ACCEPT "DON'T WANTS"

For most of us, the drift from what we want started young. As kids, we aren't always given choices based on what we want—we're often presented with the lesser of two dislikes and taught to be grateful.

I remember wanting a Big Wheel so badly it hurt. If you grew up in the '70s, you know exactly what I'm talking about—that plastic trike with the huge front wheel, small rear wheels, and handlebars with streamers that rustled in the wind. Every suburban street had them scattered across front yards. Kids would race down sidewalks, pedaling furiously, building speed to perform epic power slides. No helmets, no safety equipment, just you and the trike and the cement. You rode in "biker groups" trying to outdo each other. It was the envy of every kid.

I asked for one constantly. But like so many other times, that's not what I received. Instead, I got a strange version—the Radio Flyer Cyclone. Basically two large wheels connected to a circular plastic tube that you had to use your arms to "pedal." Instead of epic power slides and tricks, you had the choice of moving forward or spinning in circles. You couldn't keep up with the Big Wheel kids. You stood out—and not in a good way.

While it was fun, it was a "don't want" moment. I knew my options: Accept it or have nothing. Telling my parents "thanks but no thanks" wasn't possible. So, I learned to be gracious, to look excited, to push down the disappointment.

Birthdays and Christmases became glaring moments of receiving "don't want" items. Many gifts were practical—underwear, socks—because my parents believed if you were spending money, it needed to be on things you needed, not wanted. As a kid, you're more intuitive than most give you credit for. I vaguely remember being asked what I wanted for these holidays, yet there was an uneasy feeling about asking, especially for expensive items. I honestly don't recall ever getting "the" gift I truly wanted. Sometimes I'd see the wrapped presents and feel that uneasy pit in my stomach. What if it's another year of disappointment? What if it isn't what I wanted or anything close?

I learned to be gracious and accept the "don't want" because I didn't have another choice.

## HOW "DON'T WANT" THINKING CREATES THE "MORE" TRAP

It's not uncommon to live in a "don't want" space for a long time. Perhaps you haven't realized this until right now. But know that this could be a key driver in the "more" effect.

A lifetime of living in "don't want" creates unconscious accumulation. You receive something, you accept it, yet it isn't fulfilling your desires or needs. You aren't sure why, but there's an empty void this accumulation hasn't filled. Unfortunately, because you're detached from your true "want," you continue repeating the cycle of accepting other "don't wants" along the way.

This is how "don't want" thinking traps you in the accumulation cycle. You fill the void with substitutes, hoping one of them will finally satisfy, but they never do. So, you keep accumulating, searching for the thing you won't name.

## THE SCIENCE BEHIND "DON'T WANT" THINKING

Why is understanding this so important? Because we're conditioned to think in "don't wants"—I don't want to fail, I don't want to get hurt, I don't want to look stupid, I don't want to be broke, I don't want to be like my abusive parent, I don't want to be overweight. We hear and live in the "don't" in many areas of our life. You may find yourself unconsciously navigating through life and business focused on what you don't want because you're familiar with it. There are two critical considerations when you're living in that space.

Your focus and attention create your reality by directing and influencing your energy. By deciding where to place your attention, you influence the things you attract into your life and the outcomes you experience. According to this principle, your focus on what you don't want will only attract more of that to you. I like to say, "What you pay attention to, pays attention back to you." If you're paying attention to the "don't," that's what will pay you a visit.

Second, your brain doesn't recognize negatives. When you say, "I don't want to be poor," the brain hears, "I want to be poor." The subconscious can't process the word "don't." When you don't want to think about something, you do. Try this: Close your eyes for 15 seconds and whatever you do, don't think of a pink elephant.

How many times did you think about the pink elephant? "I'm not supposed to be thinking of the pink elephant. Wait, there are no pink elephants. Why did he say that? I've never seen a pink elephant. Why am I thinking about pink elephants?"

These considerations create a version of you that becomes a magnet for the "don't want" life. If we focus on what we don't want, our energy flows to it and attracts it back to us. We also attract what we don't want simply by using "don't" in our commands.

## THE TREASURE MAP: HOW "DON'TS" REVEAL YOUR WANTS

Here's the good news: Throughout my coaching, when clients struggle to articulate what they want, I've discovered that their "don't wants" become a treasure trove of invaluable information. It's actually a map to their desired future if they knew how to read it.

We've spent so much time rehearsing, repeating our dislikes, frustrations, and deal-breakers, that we can typically rattle them off with ease. This may seem negative based on what you've learned so far, but it's actually a tremendous starting point for discovering your true wants.

By taking each "don't want" statement and flipping it into its opposite, you can begin to reveal the true desire within.

For example:

"I don't want my business to be stuck at the same revenue year after year" becomes "I intend to scale my business to $1M in annual revenue with systems that support sustainable growth."

"I don't want my business to control my every waking hour" becomes "I want to design a business that runs efficiently so I can work no more than 30 hours a week and still hit my income goals."

A simple shift from avoidance language to creation language moves you from a defensive posture to a visionary one—where your true "wants" emerge and become achievable.

If you've lost sight of your true desires, spend time making a list of all your "don't wants." I promise you, they will spill off your tongue so quickly you may not be able to keep up. In fact, I often have clients grab their phone and create an audio note of their "don't wants," then go back and write them down later.

This simple yet powerful exercise will bring so much clarity in a way that feels refreshing. If you're like most, you haven't given yourself permission to live into your wants in a very long time. Once you have your list of "don'ts," use creation language to turn them around and uncover your true desires.

## THE WANT ADVANTAGE: HOW CLARITY ACCELERATES SUCCESS

When you know what you do want, it provides your brain with a GPS and a destination. Your brain takes your lead, and when you feed it the "don't" or the "do," you set the path in motion. Think of it like the GPS in your car or phone. You enter a destination in the system, and the path is revealed to you.

It's the exact same thing when you share your want with your brain. Suddenly, it knows where to go and starts looking for things to support this desire. It will see opportunities it may have ignored without your guidance and direction. You also show up differently—more focused, more intentional. Before you know it, things will "magically" appear. You may call them coincidences; I call them synchronicities.

I don't believe in coincidences. I firmly believe you're constantly cocreating your life with the universe, God, or whatever higher power resonates with you. When you're clear on your path, you experience the "flow" of life—with things falling easily into place, you don't feel like you're forcing them to happen but, instead, lighter and less stressed.

This clarity also reduces the "more" because you're clear on what you're accumulating and why. Much of the time, clearing the space allows your true desires to emerge. In moments of clarity, you may also realize some of the "more" you've picked up along the way. If they're material things, you may find yourself seeing them as "noise" and have the urge to delete them. If it's something related to career or life decisions, you may realize you're off track, that you've done things due to lack of clarity, and use this as a moment to get in alignment.

## MY JOURNEY TO GENERAL MANAGER

I remember being a manager at Marriott's Reservation Center in Omaha, Nebraska. I knew that one day I wanted my own hotel and the ability to run it as a general manager—fulfilling my longtime vision to create experiences for all guests who checked in, regardless of whether it was for work, vacation, or just a change of scenery.

This "want" was crystal clear. To make it come to life, I needed to get to a hotel and work at the property level. I met with my mentors, Dale and Klayton, and we had a very candid conversation about what that career path could look like. This clarity around my "want" lit a fire like I'd never experienced before. We mapped out my journey to general manager. At times it felt daunting, yet the "want" was so clear that I saw beyond the "how" and embraced the challenge.

I immediately put the plan in motion, and as they say, the rest is history—I became a general manager of my own hotel within five years. It wasn't as simple as just wanting to do it, but the clarity carried me through challenging times. It kept me from becoming distracted with zigzags in my career to "get more." It kept me on task, and I achieved my dreams.

It was a great example of "less being a multiplier of more" because I turned down several opportunities that were presented to me—opportunities I didn't really want but, to be honest, came with enticing financial rewards. That clarity of my true want kept me from accumulating a "don't want" career.

## THE COST OF VAGUE WANTS

One of the key elements to turning your "don't wants" to "wants" is having abundant clarity and a clear definition of your want. Vague wants like "I want to be successful" or "I want more money" are almost as unhelpful as your "don't wants."

Clarity is power. Tony Robbins teaches us this, sharing that the more clear you are about exactly what you want, the more your brain knows how to get there.

One of my mentors heard me proudly proclaim my want of making more money. I simply said, "I want to make more money this year." She walked over to me and handed me a dollar bill. She smiled and said, "There, your want of making more money this year has been achieved."

I immediately started to challenge her, and she pointed out that my "want" was vague and she officially could have met my want by giving me a penny. That lesson has stuck with me all these years later. The clearer the want, the greater the chance of achieving it.

Unclear or vague wants also confuse others. If you can't clearly express what you want, you make it harder for others to help you. Whether it's your team, your sphere of influence, or even potential clients, unclear desires lead to misaligned actions. People want to help, but they need clarity to do so effectively.

Imagine telling your team, "I don't want low engagement" versus "I want our team to create our next campaign to generate 5,000 interactions by the end of the month." The second statement immediately creates space for creativity, potential strategies, and collaborative energy.

## THE FAR-REACHING IMPACT OF KNOWING WHAT YOU WANT

Great leaders know exactly what they want, and this knowledge spills out to everyone in their organizations. Sharing specific wants is a tremendous gift to give your teams. Your team knows exactly what success looks like and can take ownership in helping you achieve it. Your clients feel more secure because your direction is steady and decisive. Your partners can align their efforts and resources with yours, creating a state of synergy instead of confusion.

The clarity of your wants extends well beyond you and your team; it also affects your brand. When you consistently express your wants, you shape a reputation for being intentional, visionary, and results oriented. This attracts like-minded people and opportunities, creating a cycle of momentum and growth.

## WANT VERSUS NEED: FINDING THE BALANCE

I think about my parents, who lived a life of need versus want. Yes, they had their share of doing things they didn't want to do to support our family, but they had clarity on the difference between a want and a need. I believe this clarity came from being first-generation Americans and products of the Great Depression. They would buy things and reflect on functionality versus meeting a "want." A car was meant to last until the wheels fell off. Shoes were meant to be functional for all occasions. You repaired worn items versus buying new replacements.

True story: When my mom was pregnant with me, my dad promised her a new car if she had a boy. Being a man of his word, he bought her a brand new 1967 *red* Dodge Coronet. She *loved* that car. It became part of her identity. Everyone knew when they saw the rusted-out Dodge coming at them, it was my mom! To my horror, she kept that car until the wheels literally fell off!

In fact, one winter day presented a distinct moment that she showed her commitment to keeping things until they stopped working! We were driving, and she needed to put either the heat or the defroster on. I saw her reach for the long-handled ice scraper in the back seat (if you are from snow country you can imagine the brush on one side and the squeegee/scraper on the other). This "scraper" became her tool to switch the buttons on the temperature control panel. She took the scraper and used it to *mash* down the button. I remember watching this unfold and thinking, *Please dear Lord, don't let anyone around us see what is happening!* Once again, it still worked! (Note, this is the same car I learned to drive when I turned 16—yes, it was still running, and it ran for many more years to come!) My mom, the MacGyver of her time, carried a few "hacks" to use on the engine to get it started when it failed. Those "tools" were a clothespin and screwdriver. She'd pop open the hood and fiddle and then *boom*, the car started and off we went.

In many ways, I envy my parents' focus on needs versus wants. In other ways, I carry a level of guilt when I give myself permission to "want" something just for the sake of the joy it will bring into my life. Whenever I take a vacation, my first thought upon arriving is, "I wish my parents would have allowed themselves to experience things like this versus denying themselves." I wonder what they would have thought of the beautiful hotel room, the new experiences and the memories created. I've learned to appreciate a balance, honoring that "wants" aren't a bad thing if they serve a purpose versus accumulation of "more." I honor that I'm congruent with my "wants" in all areas of my life and that those wants serve a purpose.

Once you've identified your wants, make sure you spend time reviewing them. Find the purpose of those wants to flush out any remnant of doing it for the sake of "more." Allow yourself to enjoy the pursuit of a want that adds value to your life, business, finances, or relationships. Don't confuse honoring a want for the sake of "more" versus honoring a want that enhances your true life.

Less is the great multiplier of more, and this is also true in the want versus "don't want" category.

## PERMISSION TO WANT

High school, college, and my first few jobs were uneventful and the byproduct of my "don't wants." I knew I didn't want to live at home any longer—not for any negative reason other than I wanted to start my life. I took a few jobs I truly didn't want, but they provided the financial resources to move.

It wasn't until I had amazing mentors to guide me that I could give myself permission to admit what I wanted—to stop taking jobs, advice, and opportunities that were great but misaligned with my wants. I'm forever grateful for their guidance because my life unfolded in ways I might have never been able to see.

You see, I was raised to be grateful for what was "given" to you and not reject it. To be humble and accepting of opportunities that were presented. To not challenge them by checking if they were in alignment with my true wants. In my home, stating what you wanted was viewed as arrogant or impolite. It was just the programming my parents were given, and they passed it to me.

When I learned to turn my don't wants into wants, I turned those wants into my life's vision and mission: I want to live a financially abundant life and create true financial freedom (do what I want, when I want, with whom I want). I want to live a big life and create experiences for myself, my family, and my friends. I want to run my own company where I get to say what's allowed and what's not a good idea.

The fact that this is my current life is a direct result of such clarity.

## YOUR TURN: THE WANT REVOLUTION

Go back to your "don't wants" list and put some energy behind those thoughts. Make them come to life as your "wants." Allow yourself to feel the energy shift, to see the impact, and to envision your life as you truly want it to be.

This isn't about becoming selfish or materialistic. It's about reclaiming the muscle of desiring that's been dormant for too long. It's about giving yourself permission to be clear about your path so you can stop accumulating "don't wants" disguised as "more."

In a blink, we're conditioned to accept "don't wants" in life. It starts at an early age, and over time—gradually, then suddenly—you may have forgotten to express your true wants regularly. The impact of accepting "don't wants" can be a significant factor in your world of "more." More isn't a bad thing as long as it's the right more, not the default more.

Living in the space of "don't want" will actually attract more of it into your life, business, and relationships. Energy flows where attention goes, and if you're unclear about your true wants, you'll give more attention and energy to what you don't want.

There's a distinct advantage to clarity around your "wants." It provides a map to your brain to seek out and find what you truly do want. You'll be crystal clear on the direction, and the path will unfold. The good news on your journey to clarity is that your "don't wants" leave clues, and what you do want is typically the opposite of what you don't.

Use creation language versus avoidance language to find your way. Moving forward in your "want zone" will accelerate your success and make every decision easier and more powerful. You'll have discovered your true north; when you follow it, you'll have new energy and new possibilities. It allows you to live in less fear, less worry, less resentment, and less frustration.

Learn the difference between true wants and needs. Wanting things for the right reason adds value to your life, business, and relationships. It helps you eliminate the noise, live in the "less," and receive the effects of "less is the great multiplier of more."

The question "What do you want?" doesn't have to be terrifying anymore. It can be the beginning of everything you've been searching for while accumulating everything you don't want. Your "don't wants" have been whispering your truth all along. It's time to listen.

## LESS OVER MORE: KEY INSIGHTS

- **"Don't wants" are treasure maps to true desires:** Every frustration and complaint is actually a clue pointing to what you do want—flip avoidance language into creation language to discover your path.
- **Your brain can't process negatives:** When you say, "I don't want to be poor," your brain hears, "I want to be poor." What you focus on expands, so focusing on "don'ts" attracts more unwanted experiences.
- **Vague wants create the "more" trap:** "I want to be successful" or "I want more money" are as unhelpful as "don't wants"—clarity is power, and specific wants accelerate success while preventing accumulation.
- **Clear wants create magnetic focus:** When you know exactly what you want, your brain becomes a GPS seeking opportunities to support that desire, creating the "flow" where synchronicities appear naturally.
- **Permission to want isn't selfish, it's essential:** Reclaiming the muscle of desiring after years of accepting "don't wants" is how you stop accumulating substitutes and start building the life you actually want.

## CHAPTER 13

# THE RIGHT MORE AND THE RIGHT LESS

You've come a long way on this journey. You've examined your relationship with "more," explored the science behind your thoughts, learned to say no, curated your relationships, redefined your relationship with money, and discovered what you truly want. You've done the hard work of recognizing where "more" has quietly taken over your life.

Here's the question that matters most: How do you actually live this? How do you maintain the clarity you've gained? And perhaps most importantly, how do you tell the difference between the "right more" and the "wrong more"?

Because here's what I need you to understand: Remember, this isn't about deprivation. This isn't about quitting your job, abandoning your salary, or walking away from the career or business you've built over years. It's about finding the rhythm and balance of "less" and recognizing the "more" it can create.

Less is the great multiplier of more. Not sometimes. Always.

## THE REALITY YOU'RE LIVING

Let me remind you of where many of us are right now (thank you to author Joshua Becker, in his blog post,[34] for bringing these to my attention):

- The average American has over 300,000 items in their home.[35]
- The average size of the American home has nearly tripled over the past 50 years.[36]
- One out of every 10 Americans rents off-site storage.[37]

Maybe your position of "more" has occurred simply because it's become the norm in our belief system. You've become numb to your reality. When you're in an accumulation state, gathering things like job titles, houses, cars, jewelry, designer handbags to validate your current state, it happens gradually, then suddenly. You probably weren't even aware you'd arrived in this state of "more" as you enter a state of numbness to the reality of what you are doing. Over time, you lose sight of the impact.

The important thing to realize is it has happened.

Joshua Fields Millburn and Ryan Nicodemus, dubbed "The Minimalists," say that "minimalism is a tool that can assist you in finding freedom. Freedom from fear. Freedom from worry. Freedom from overwhelm. Freedom from guilt. Freedom from depression. Freedom from the trappings of the consumer culture we've built our lives around. Real freedom."[38]

If I'm completely honest with myself, I have everything I need to survive and thrive. Unlike Josh Fields who states he has only 288 items in his home,[39] I'd venture to say I have way more than 288 items, yet I've pared my belongings down significantly and have gone from many things to fewer, higher-quality things.

For example, art. We're fortunate to live in Santa Fe, where we have access to some of the world's best art. I have a rule: If I find a piece of art I want to add to our collection, I must decide which piece I'm going to eliminate to make room for this new find. Most of the time, I pass on the new piece and remember that I have more than enough. I typically return home, reflect on the amazing pieces I already have, and think about the talented local artists who created the masterpieces I'm fortunate enough to own.

Where in your life are you accumulating? Where has the "gradually" become suddenly, and you have more than you need? Is it clothing? Handbags? Cars? Where could you use a cleansing toward "less" that would allow you to have more meaningful things?

In my "less" life, the space for more shows up every day—more appreciation, more gratitude, more peace, more joy. As the noise and distractions lessen, I also have space for more creativity.

## WHAT "LESS" REALLY MEANS

Many people view "less" as being in a place of scarcity or lack. The reality is that's not the truth, though it can be perceived that way. This perception is what keeps people trapped in "more"—they're afraid that choosing less means settling or choosing deprivation or limitation.

Nothing could be further from the truth.

"More" can define your belief in abundance. You may associate living an abundant life with the "things" you have, the job titles you hold, the external markers of success. And you're not alone in this thinking—it's what we've all been taught.

But what if abundance isn't measured by accumulation? What if true abundance is measured by space—space for what matters, space for opportunities you can't yet see, space for the life you actually want to live?

When I finally got over my perceived image of "less" and began embracing this new definition, I started feeling lighter. There was an unmistakable feeling of things being easier. I constantly felt like things were just showing up, and I was in the flow. It allowed for amazing opportunities and the natural end of things that no longer served my higher needs.

## THE PROOF: WHEN SPACE CREATES MIRACLES

One of the best examples of what space can provide is this book. I've thought about writing a book for years, but I didn't have space in my schedule to make it happen. In fact, there was always a reason not to do it. I'd pick up a few more clients to build my roster. I'd write another group coaching program that required time and effort to launch, market, and fulfill. I'd say yes to projects that were out of alignment but provided "more" income, "more" attention, "more" fulfillment of my need for significance.

When I finally got serious about rightsizing my own business and letting go of things that were my "more," I had space for this opportunity. "Less" was opening up doors to "more."

I believe I had a series of divine moments that led to me having the capacity to write this book. It was as if domino after domino was dropping into my life in perfect timing, providing the path to Less Over More. I could not have written a better plan.

The first domino fell when my dear friend Suzanne started nudging me—okay, pushing, prodding, and maybe insisting—that I write this book. Suzanne then had a random, unplanned meeting with my agent. She told him about me and what I was considering. He reached out and agreed to take on this project. We quickly found ourselves in alignment, and I began the journey.

The surprises kept coming. A chance opportunity with a brilliant former peer aligned my coaching company with the company he's leading, providing the leverage I needed to give this book my attention while continuing to grow my coaching business in the right direction. And finally, I was presenting at a local mastermind group where the incredible author Tania Katan was speaking. She saw an opportunity and graciously reached out for us to work together.

I hadn't been seeking any of these opportunities. All "magically" showed up. All continued to reinforce that this was the right direction at the right time. One of my affirmations—"*Right here, right now, everything is lining up for the life I'm meant to live*"—was coming true right before my eyes.

Had I not cleared the space and moved into true alignment, I believe none of this would have happened. This book may have never come to fruition.

Is it possible that we have no idea of the amazing things just waiting for us to make space so they can show up and enhance our lives? That we're unconsciously blocking and robbing ourselves of our truest joy? That we are potentially the greatest barrier to our ultimate success when we block our truest blessings with our perceived concept of "more"?

What have you always wanted to do but never had time for? What have you found yourself making excuses around that's keeping you from your truest opportunities? When was the last time you allowed space in your business, life, and relationships to see what's possible?

## THE RIGHT MORE VERSUS THE WRONG MORE

Is there such a thing as the "right more"? Absolutely. My goal is not to have you shift into a mindset that "more" is bad or negative. It's not. It's important to know the difference between the "right" more and the "wrong" more.

I can't stress enough: More is a beautiful thing, provided it's the right more. The right more may feel foreign to you because it's a new way of thinking, acting, and receiving. The "wrong more" fulfilled a different set of needs—you were making decisions out of alignment with your core values and accepting it as your fate. You saw your wrong more as an opportunity to get ahead and show the world you're rocking it. You accumulated things and took opportunities for the sake of image, looking good, and being right—a true human condition.

For me, knowing it's the right "more" is simple: It's immediately congruent with my values and feels natural and unforced. I'm not forcing something to happen or trying to make something "fit" into my business, life, or relationship—you know, square peg, round hole.

I'm also not saying it's easy when I choose the right "more," but it's worth it because that more has an energy of excitement, possibility, and joy. Many of my "right more" moments required incredible attention, effort, and even failure, but I'm driven to continue because I feel it deep in my soul. I believe wholeheartedly that I'm on the right path, and many signs appear that confirm I'm indeed on it.

As author Caroline Myss beautifully told Oprah Winfrey in her 2012 interview on *Super Soul Sunday*, when asked how to know whether you're on the right path: "Here's your clue . . . You're not put in a position where you feel like you have to negotiate your sense of integrity, which is an act of betrayal . . . You don't feel like you have to compromise who you are."[40]

## THE SIGNAL YOU CAN'T IGNORE: EXHAUSTION AND BURNOUT

How do you know if you're living in the "wrong more"? One of the easiest signs is that you're experiencing exhaustion and burnout. If you think about it, how couldn't you be? You've most likely drifted from your values and are operating in a space that's out of alignment.

After I resigned from my corporate job and took a moment to clear some space, the magic started to happen. I wasn't exactly sure what I was going to do next because I'd never allowed myself the time to reflect on what I wanted. In the time I was allowed to recover and clear space, it became crystal clear that I'd always wanted to be a Realtor but had never allowed that "want" to be more than a fleeting thought.

What I found out is that being a Realtor aligned 100% with my vision and values. As they say, the rest is history—a fabulous and amazing history that ultimately led me to coaching and the life I have the privilege of living now.

Take a moment and check in with yourself. Are you feeling exhausted and on the verge of burnout—or already in the storm of it? You may not be consciously aware of this, which is why it's critical to check in on your status from time to time. In your business, life, or relationships, are you feeling off balance? Out of sync or just "off" for no reason?

## THE PIVOT: MAKING YOUR "MORE" WORK FOR YOU

Is there an easy button to press to get to the "right less"? Everyone's journey is unique and different. Some have to get to the point of being "sick and tired of being sick and tired" to feel it, while others may have a moment of clarity that it's time to do something different. Remember, mine was the "hood of the car moment."

Switching to "less" can seem like an extreme swing of the pendulum. This movement to "less" is not a battle cry to quit or have a knee-jerk reaction to your current situation. I'm not endorsing making changes without a plan; rather, explore first what impact it will have on your business, life, wealth, and relationships.

Is it possible to make your "wrong more" less wrong? Yes. Many of us arrive at a place in business and life where we realize the drift from our values and goals left us in a place we wouldn't choose again. Other than completely abandoning your job, life, or relationship, which I don't recommend or endorse, you can assess what you can do to bring things into alignment.

Can we make your current "more" work for you? The answer is yes. The first step is grace. Embrace imperfection and allow yourself to stay out of judgment. Judging or being overly critical of yourself won't allow the space for you to move forward. You made the best decisions with the knowledge you had at the time. None of your decisions were made with the intention of picking the "wrong more."

Next, assess where you are and gain clarity. Review all duties and responsibilities of your current position and start with the positive— what's in alignment? Then identify what's out of alignment. What are you doing that you no longer need to do? What can you replace those things with that would add value and be in alignment?

I had a client facing exactly this situation. Her alignment was to be more in sales versus operations, so we explored what she could do to incorporate sales into her current role. The process needed to be gradual, beginning with becoming a liaison between operations and sales, creating a bridge to gain understanding between the two divisions. Little by little, the sales team viewed her as a critical source and began including her in their strategy meetings. Over time, a new position was created for her that allowed her to move into a role in sales that was a substantial promotion. The job description seemed to have "written itself" to be in total alignment with her values.

Consider whether you can leverage or offboard things that aren't in alignment. If this is a corporate role, you may need to create a solid plan of what you're recommending to change in your role and the positive impact it will have on your corporation.

Ask yourself: Can I alter what I'm doing that's not in alignment and bring it into alignment? Is there a career move I can make out of my current role into one more in alignment? This may not be an overnight move and may take the support of those you work with. Revisit the organizational chart and see if there's a more appropriate role for you. If there is, what's the path to get there?

The last option to consider is your exit strategy. If you realize there's no option to realign, is it time to look outside your current employer? And here's something interesting: Is it possible that if you do some of the preceding work, you'll create space for an amazing internal opportunity to appear?

## LIVING THE MULTIPLIER EFFECT

Clients often hear me say, "Less is the great multiplier of more." It's one of my favorite things to say because it acts as a pattern interrupt. It jostles their brain and makes them pause and question what I'm saying. I firmly believe it's the truth, though many will push back and challenge my belief. They have no concept that less can bring them more. They're living in a world of old programming that's taught us that if we want more, we must do more.

But we can only do "more" for a set amount of time before we become tired, weary, and potentially full of doubt.

Consider this: The time of greatest motivation is when you're setting a goal. You get to predict the wonderful future you're going to experience, what you're going to "have" in the end. Then you have to get busy and make it happen. Stephen Covey famously taught us the "Be, Do, Have" concept—you must first embody the person who holds the outcome you desire (Be), then take actions aligned with that identity (Do), and when you achieve those, you reach the Have.

Creating "more" ignites the "have" feeling in all of us. We get incredibly motivated about what "more" can allow us to have. The problem? The excitement of doing "more" wears off quickly—usually by 7 PM that night or within a day or two—because we're pushing ourselves in one area only: "Do more."

Consider the Thought Flow Model we explored earlier. The results you achieve depend on actions, but actions depend on feelings, energy, and emotions triggered by thoughts. If we solely focus on the "action" aspect, we most likely won't improve our results, at least not long term. It's the thoughts and feelings that really drive that bus.

You may not have to do more if you address those two things. Clearing your thoughts, reframing them, and retraining them is a form of clearing and venturing into "less." You're releasing old thoughts that are holding you back, limiting beliefs that are hijacking your true success. New and empowering thoughts take up less space and can have the greatest impact on achieving your results.

One of my favorite clients was taking over his mother's business. He was no stranger to leadership and business strategies, but somewhere along the way, he lost sight of the "less" that would bring him the greatest success. He was fortunate to have taken over a business with a robust database—one large enough that on its own could get him and his team to their goal.

When we cleared the "more" he was engaging in, cleared the path, and gained clarity that 100% focus on his database could get him to his goal, everything changed. Initially, it felt odd to step away from other sources of lead generation and growth to trust that his database would drive him to success. But in less than 90 days of doing "less," he was receiving more. It was also more enjoyable and allowed him to be a better spouse, dad, son, and brother. It improved how he was able to show up in life and achieve the goals he'd created.

## THE JOURNEY CONTINUES

As much as I'd love to proclaim I've fully evolved, I'm still human with a human brain that likes to quietly lull me back to where it feels comfortable, even when comfortable isn't the highest form of my "less" life.

This is why it is important to do frequent check-ins with yourself. Are you falling into old habits? Have you started taking on the "wrong more" again? Do things feel out of alignment?

Imagine your experience being like driving a car that's out of alignment. You can drive, but you're constantly course-correcting to stay between the lines. It requires much more effort, and honestly isn't as enjoyable. This is exactly what's happening to so many people, yet they've become numb to the fact that it's no longer enjoyable or easy and is becoming increasingly difficult to live between the lines.

But when you get into alignment—when you clear the space and choose the "right more"—everything changes. Things become easier. Opportunities appear. The path unfolds. You experience flow.

And that flow? That's not magic. That's what happens when less becomes the great multiplier of more.

## LESS OVER MORE: KEY INSIGHTS

- **Less is the great multiplier of more:** Clearing space doesn't create deprivation—it creates room for opportunities you can't yet see, like dominoes falling in perfect timing to bring your dreams to life.
- **"Right more" energizes, "wrong more" exhausts:** If you're experiencing burnout and feeling drained, you're likely seeking the "wrong more"—out of alignment with your values and forcing things that don't fit naturally.
- **You don't have to abandon everything to pivot:** Assess what's in alignment versus out of alignment, leverage or offboard misaligned tasks, and create a plan to shift gradually toward work that aligns with your vision.
- **The 300,000-item trap is real:** The average American accumulates this much because "more" has become the norm. Recognizing your accumulation pattern is the first step to breaking free.
- **Thoughts drive results more than actions:** Instead of doing more, clear and reframe your thoughts. New, empowering thoughts take up less space and create greater impact than endless action ever could.

## CHAPTER 14

# MAKING YOUR LESS YOUR MORE

One of my favorite reframe phrases is simply "What if" followed by a positive result. When I do this, I open my brain to think of all that is truly possible. I focus on the results and not the "how." The how will show up on a need-to-know basis; for now, I just trust in the intention and results. This is one of those phrases I use when I am allowing a disempowering thought to enter my mind. I turn "What if I fail?" into "What if I succeed?" Doing this immediately reclaims my power and resets my potential.

> *What if your dreams become your reality? What if you find peace, joy, and happiness? What if you live the life you have always wanted and receive More Through Less?*

It was early 2005 when I was introduced to this concept of "Making the What If . . . What Is™." I was four years into my real estate career and experiencing tremendous success. Much of this was because of my previous corporate experience and the fact that I was treating my business like a business. I saw others struggling and felt a desire to help them find their way. I often thought, "what if" I could help those new and seasoned agents clear a path to success? I spoke with my broker and pitched the idea of me providing a two-day training program, and they were beyond excited to have this as part of their curriculum.

Once they approved it, I realized I hadn't created a program quite like this and would need some help. Enter, Beth Paul! Beth was a dear friend and a talented presenter and course writer. I'd met Beth in my previous life at Marriott and knew she could help.

We sat at my kitchen table and began writing the program. In the process, she said, "You do realize you made your 'what if,' your 'what is.'" I paused and asked her to explain.

She said I had a desire, my "what if I could help" that I'd now made my "what is." In typical Beth brilliance, "Making the What If . . . What Is™" came to life. This became my anthem, and eventually the tagline for my coaching company. This was also my first "taste" of creating the space for amazing things to happen with a simple thought. I hadn't really given much consideration to the "how," and when the broker said yes to the program, it was showtime. This thought came to life and created a new opportunity for me in my real estate career, one in total alignment with my values. Thoughts truly do drive all results. This was the beginning of something *big* in my life.

## THE POWER OF INTENTION

Your authentic life is waiting for you! First you must trust the process outlined in this book. It deviates from what many of us have been conditioned to believe and from how the world has shaped our beliefs. I think one of the most challenging things to do when you are creating the space for more is to trust the process. To have faith that there is a different way and that it can and will work for you. You are definitely a product of your environment, and you may have blindly ambled forward on your journey, innocently playing into the beliefs of others. Doing what was expected of you and what met the standards and expectations of society. When you reclaim your beliefs and potential, things start to change. One of my favorite quotes that emphasizes your possibility is:

> The number one principle that rules my life is intention. Thought by thought, choice by choice, we are cocreating our lives based on the energy of our intention.
>
> —Oprah Winfrey, *The Wisdom of Sundays*

What is your intention? What is your ultimate desire? You see, once you embrace this, you get to cocreate your life with God, the universe, a higher power, or whatever you believe in. How exciting this concept is. You don't "blindly follow"—you actually get to partner in the creation of the life you want. Let go of what the world expects and wants from you and take a stand for what is important to you!

## WHEN BELIEFS WANE

If you truly are going to clear space and allow things to show up, you must have a degree of trust and belief in the process. At first, it may seem risky or a bit "woo-woo"; however, there are far too many examples of this working for it to not have possibility. Remember, your brain is going to do its best to keep you safe and consistent in your old ways. Key to overcoming this and pursuing your "less" life are your beliefs.

A belief is a form of a thought, like "I believe I will be a millionaire." Now, for some, this is a great fantasy; yet when they strive to actually believe it, they are filled with thoughts that create doubt and disbelief: "Who do you think you are? No one in your family has ever been wealthy. You don't have the skills to do anything to make a million. You don't operate in those circles. You aren't 'those' people. You aren't smart enough. You are too old. There is too much competition in the space you operate. There isn't enough to go around." I'm exhausted just saying those things, yet those *thoughts* will kill the believability of that belief.

Lean into the Thought Flow Model and the Four Questions to redirect your thoughts. This model helps turn the disempowering thought around and replace it with an empowering and believable thought. You get to take the thought out of your unconscious mind and acknowledge it, reframe it, and create the thought you'd prefer to have. Remember, thoughts drive all results, and catching the disempowering thought the moment you feel it is the *secret* to changing everything.

## LIVING IN YOUR FUTURE

When was the last time you allowed yourself to live in your future? This is where we get to explore our truest desires. Think of your future as the place you can have everything you desire—an Amazon for your future! All you need to do is search for it, see it, and order it. Your life dreams, business dreams, wealth dreams, and relationship dreams are all living within your grasp and can be as easy as "ordering them up." It is all there, just waiting for you.

Our future fades because most of us spend too much time reflecting on what we didn't do or did wrong (past) and what we are currently doing (now) but *rarely* allow ourselves time in our future. Your future is the place where you can see the things that you want to receive. Creating this vision of the future is a critical element in receiving your future desires, by spending time living in the future and feeling and experiencing it in your mind—letting yourself experience all the "feel goods" that come from achieving and receiving what you desire—as if it has already happened!

As I mentioned in chapter 7, a powerful way to create this is to write a letter dated in the future: "Today is December 31, 2028. I am so grateful for the life and business I have created. Looking at my savings account balance of $2,500,000 gives me such peace. I'm signing the last of the bonus checks for my team—the pride I have for their accomplishments is beyond anything I imagined. I'm excited to give my family their passports for our dream European vacation, knowing I've paid for it in full and the memories we'll create . . ."

You see, when you create the story that you are living in the future, your brain will actually release all those feel-good hormones and find peace in knowing that this is where you intend to be. It is an incredible way to realize your "Be, Do, Have."

## WHAT IF = WANT?

For so long, you may have lived in the space of experiencing and accepting your "don't want." This may be the first time you have given yourself permission to acknowledge your "want." We are on a journey to make your true wants in business, life, and relationships into your new reality.

Take a moment and let that sink in. Take a deep breath and live into your wants. Live into the possibility that this book, its resources, and its tools have created a path for you to experience less and therefore, the *right* more.

What "want" has been stifled for you? Pushed down and ignored? You are now giving it permission to emerge for you. Will you allow yourself the space to create the path toward it? What do you need to clear to open yourself up to experience it?

## SAYING YES MEANS SAYING NO

On your journey of rightsizing your business, life, wealth, and relationships, it is critical to know that when you say yes to one thing, you are saying no to something else. Saying "yes" to the right more is saying "no" to the wrong more, which is the space in which great things will happen for you! This is a key piece of migrating from more to less. Make sure you haven't crowded the space for your rightsizing to come true because you have said yes to so many other things.

Early on, I realized that I was always the person others came to—bosses, clients, friends—when they needed something done. I always felt really good about helping, yet what I wasn't aware of was that each time I said yes to one of their needs, I was unconsciously saying no to mine. I was filling the space with others' dreams, visions, and tasks, and crowding mine out. I was doing "more," but it was not the "right more" for me. Funny thing, I truly believed that saying no to them would hinder my success. The truth is, when I started saying no, it created the space for me to have more success and flourish. No one ever got annoyed with me for saying no. They appreciated the boundary and knew I would do it if I could.

## THE ENERGY OF LESS

Remember, less is not about lack or scarcity. It is what wrings out the sponge of opportunity in your business, life, wealth, and relationships. It is one of the purest gifts you can give to yourself to experience true joy and peace.

Doing less reduces friction, stress, and decision fatigue. Reclaiming this energy becomes rocket fuel for the things that move your dream forward, transforming wishful thinking into lived reality. When you are focused on the right more, your energy is different, almost contagious. When you are focused on the wrong "more," your energy is scattered—and scattered energy produces scattered results. Intentional energy produces exponential results. When you focus less on many and more on the few, your future stops being someday—it starts being now!

I'm not saying that your new path will be easy. In fact, it can be quite the contrary. Any time you start a new venture, you are faced with new challenges and unknown opportunities. However, when you are in alignment and *finally* have said yes to the right more, you enter the flow! The space where things seem easier, the pieces fit, the future looks oh so bright, and synchronicities happen constantly.

For me, I know I'm in the flow when, at the end of a long day, I have abundant energy. I feel the buzz of opportunity and can hardly wait for the next day to begin! This only happens when you are entrenched in the "right more" and have had the courage to say NO to the wrong more.

A defining "less" moment for me was when I entered the world of real estate. I had left all that I knew in the hospitality industry, along with a great salary, benefits package, and the platform to create great experiences for travelers. It was an industry that I knew the ins and outs of and where I could navigate any situation with ease. Never did I imagine my entering real estate would lead me to coaching, or that this would become what I did for a living. I never even had an inkling that I would write a book to help as many people as possible to discover their Less Over More life. Becoming a Realtor opened doors that I didn't even know existed. I went from selling homes, to running a successful real estate team, to franchise ownership, to coaching, to being an author and speaker. Had I not cleared the space, I would have missed out on my incredible life. The people I have met on this journey, the clients I have the privilege of coaching, and now, this book—*wow!*

## CREATING OVERFLOW

This is the time when you must say *no* to the wrong things. If it doesn't align with your values, it is a no. If it isn't in alignment with your "right more," it is a no. Saying no to the wrong things gives the right things the space to show up.

Nothing excites me more than coaching a client to claim their "right more." To watch the impact it has on their business, lives, and relationships. To watch them light up from the inside out is one of the best feelings.

I had a client who was running a large team, collecting associates along the way to demonstrate to her peers how successful she was. She took on project after project that sapped her bandwidth of energy and joy. She said yes to opportunities because she feared if she passed on them, her competition would say yes to them and outperform her.

When we stripped it down and cleared the excess, she realized that it had been a very long time since she enjoyed her team and her business. She was exhausted and compared herself to a ball bouncing in a pinball machine between bumpers and targets; never staying in one place long enough to make a difference, yet, to the outside world, seemingly successful. Her words will forever live in my head: "I've built my dream business, yet it is a nightmare and I want *out*." She was ready to just walk away from everything to reclaim her sanity and her peace.

We quickly got to work, identifying the "more" and releasing those factors that were not in alignment or providing value. You know, the ones that were truly just taking up space. We cleared her roster as well and removed those associates who were taking more than giving and were the true source of her greatest discontent. Was she afraid to do this? *Yes!* Was it a big step to eliminate so much of what became her norm over time? *Yes!* Did more show up through the creation of less? *Yes yes yes!*

After she caught her breath and reorganized her team and actions, she immediately noticed the clients she attracted were people she actually wanted to work with. Her team members started converting more sales and had a positive attitude. It only took a few months, but in that time she cleared the space, creating an opening for the "right more" to find its way home.

Doing less with intention creates margin (the right more)—margin for joy, for peace, for relationships, and for opportunities. Once you unleash your truest intention, more shows up in a big way! You get to experience things with clarity and see them through a lens that was blocked or cloudy. Suddenly your vision is crystal clear, and you feel like you finally know what euphoria is meant to feel like.

## YOUR JOURNEY FORWARD

Like any new exercise, your journey to Less Over More may take a minute to process and implement. Liken this to muscles that you are looking to develop, for which your trainer recommends a new routine. At first, it is uncomfortable and your muscles may hurt, but after a short time, you adapt to the new routine and experience a true breakthrough in growth. The process in this book is similar in that it may feel uncomfortable at first, requiring you to persevere to get to the breakthrough.

I'd recommend you select one area in your business, life, wealth, or relationship that may not require as much change. Perhaps you want to test it in an area that feels safer to you. Build your confidence, gather evidence that it works, and then expand into other areas.

Think of all the attention and focus you are giving to the wrong "more"—or someone else's. What could moving that focus to your "more" do for you, your family, your team, and your legacy?

## BETH'S GIFT

I lost my dear friend Beth to cancer. Beth was the one who sat at my kitchen table and gave words to what would become the foundation of my life's work. She was the one who encouraged me to step into coaching, to build a life of more through less, and to pursue my version of freedom and flexibility. I do not believe I was aware that this is what she was doing and instilling, yet when I reflect back on moments in my life that made the greatest impact, this was one of them. It was a significant reminder of doing the "right more"—only what is in alignment with your core values.

Her words became more than encouragement; they became the foundation of reTHINK Coaching and my own compass for how I live and work. When I feel myself slipping into the "more" trap, I hear her voice: "You made your 'what if,' your 'what is.'" It brings me back, every single time.

This book is designed to give you the space to step into what you've always wanted—and even what you haven't yet imagined—because until now, you may not have created the room for magic to show up. Step out of the "more" and into the "less."

Please take what you've learned here and apply it. Go create, manifest, lean into Making the What If . . . What Is™—and live a *big* life of Less Over More.

Your authentic life is waiting.

# ACKNOWLEDGMENTS

Acknowledging all who had an impact on this book is an impossible task. So many people have shared their lives, stories, and personal and professional journeys with me, and for that, I am deeply grateful. My own journey has had its ups and downs, yet each step has shaped who I am today.

Before turning the page, I want to honor those who have held the greatest parts of my heart and life throughout this journey: the ones who never doubted me or discouraged me from being audacious enough to think that I could write a book. You are the ones who simply asked, "How can I help?"

- First and foremost, my faith and relationship with God. Nothing about this journey happened by chance; it was all part of His plan.
- My husband, Reagan, who at times lent me his belief in my possibilities when I needed it most.
- My two amazing sisters. There's something special about loving each other as children and something extraordinary about choosing each other as best friends in adulthood. Though we

don't live near one another, the calls, visits, texts, and connection remain as strong as ever.

- My parents. You now have the best seat in the house to watch my life unfold, to see it in a way few ever have. I have no doubt your influence has been present in this project from day one. You taught me the value of hard work, honesty, and, most importantly, how to show up in the world.
- My extended family, nieces, nephews, and in-laws. Thank you for being so genuinely excited for this phase of my life. Your enthusiasm gave lift and encouragement.
- To my front row, you know who you are. I realize now more than ever, having your own cheerleading squad is one of life's greatest gifts. Your unwavering support has never gone unnoticed. You made this venture joyful and full of love.
- Matt Holt, Jonas Koffler, and team. Your patience and guidance were a true gift. Thank you for trusting me and taking on this project.

This book may have my name on the cover, yet it was built through the love, belief, and generosity of many. I am profoundly grateful for each of you who walked beside me and with me on this journey. I hope these pages reflect even a fraction of what you have given me.

# NOTES


1. Carla Fried, "$38 Billion Is Spent Yearly on Self-Storage," *The Gazette*, January 24, 2020, https://www.thegazette.com/nation-world/38-billion-is-spent-yearly-on-self-storage/.
2. TriCore Investment Group, LinkedIn post, accessed January 28, 2026, https://www.linkedin.com/posts/tricore-investment-group_self-storage-continues-to-stand-out-as-a-activity-7412900620044562433-2LFn.
3. Clay S. Jenkinson, "Too Much Stuff: Americans and Their Storage Units," *Governing*, December 18, 2022, https://www.governing.com/context/too-much-stuff-americans-and-their-storage-units.
4. Eleanor Goldberg, "You're Probably Going to Throw Away 81 Pounds of Clothing this Year," HuffPost, June 9, 2016, https://www.huffpost.com/entry/youre-likely-going-to-throw-away-81-pounds-of-clothing-this-year_n_57572bc8e4b08f74f6c069d3.
5. "Durable Goods: Product-Specific Data," United States Environmental Protection Agency website, accessed January 28, 2026, https://www.epa.gov/facts-and-figures-about-materials-waste-and-recycling/durable-goods-product-specific-data.
6. Mary MacVean, "For Many People, Gathering Possessions Is Just the Stuff of Life," *Los Angeles Times*, March 21, 2014, https://www.latimes.com/health/la-he-keeping-stuff-20140322-story.html.

7. Taylor Covington, "Supersized: Americans Are Living in Bigger Houses with Fewer People," The Zebra, May 15, 2024, https://www.thezebra.com/resources/home/median-home-size-in-us/.

8. "Ten-Year-Olds Have £7,000 Worth of Toys but Play with Just £330," *The Telegraph*, October 20, 2010, https://www.telegraph.co.uk/finance/newsbysector/retailandconsumer/8074156/Ten-year-olds-have-7000-worth-of-toys-but-play-with-just-330.html.

9. Josh Sanburn, "America's Clutter Problem," *Time*, March 12, 2015, https://time.com/3741849/americas-clutter-problem/.

10. Emma Johnson, "The Real Cost of Your Shopping," *Forbes*, June 29, 2021, https://www.forbes.com/sites/emmajohnson/2015/01/15/the-real-cost-of-your-shopping-habits/.

11. Peter G. Stromberg, "Do Americans Consume Too Much?" *Psychology Today*, July 29, 2012, https://www.psychologytoday.com/us/blog/sex-drugs-and-boredom/201207/do-americans-consume-too-much.

12. Marie Haaland, "Americans Waste $18K on 'Nonessential' Expenses a Year," *New York Post*, May 2, 2019, https://nypost.com/2019/05/02/americans-waste-18k-on-non-essential-expenses-a-year/.

13. Roy Baumeister, "Yielding to Temptation: Self-Control Failure, Impulsive Purchasing, and Consumer Behavior," *Journal of Consumer Research* 28, no. 4 (March 2002): 670–676, doi:10.1086/338209.

14. Walter Mischel, *The Marshmallow Test: Mastering Self-Control* (Little, Brown and Co., 2014).

15. Monica Pitrelli, "Americans and Japanese Take Far Less Time Off—but Europeans Say They're More 'Vacation Deprived,'" CNBC, June 30, 2024, https://www.cnbc.com/2024/07/01/americans-take-less-time-off-but-europeans-are-more-vacation-deprived.html.

16. "Working Time Directive," accessed January 28, 2026, https://employment-social-affairs.ec.europa.eu/policies-and-activities/rights-work/labour-law/working-conditions/working-time-directive_en.

17. Kirsten Chorpenning, "Nearly 1 in 4 US Workers Took No Vacation Days (PTO Statistics 2025)," FlexJobs.com, October 14, 2025, https://www.flexjobs.com/blog/post/pto-statistics.

18. Allison Schrager, "Americans Need to Learn to Live More Like Europeans," November 12, 2021, https://www.fa-mag.com/news/americans-need-to-learn-to-live-more-like-europeans-64875.html?print.
19. "Quotes from Joseph Campbell," Joseph Campbell Foundation, accessed January 28, 2026, https://www.jcf.org/learn/quotes.
20. Erin Bluvas, "Most of Our Daily Behaviors Are Habits, According to New Research," University of South Carolina, September 23, 2025, https://sc.edu/study/colleges_schools/public_health/about/news/2025/habits_research_rebar_hpeb.php.
21. Dave Chaffey, "Global Social Media Statistics Research Summary," Smart Insights, February 14, 2025, https://www.smartinsights.com/social-media-marketing/social-media-strategy/new-global-social-media-research/.
22. Byron Katie, *Loving What Is: Four Questions That Can Change Your Life* (Three Rivers Press, 2003).
23. Fran Simone, "Negative Self-Talk: Don't Let It Overwhelm You," *Psychology Today*, December 4, 2017, https://www.psychologytoday.com/us/blog/family-affair/201712/negative-self-talk-dont-let-it-overwhelm-you.
24. C. Northcote Parkinson, "Parkinson's Law," *The Economist*, November 19, 1955, https://www.economist.com/news/1955/11/19/parkinsons-law.
25. "The 3 Words That Will Make You Rich," T. Harv Eker website, accessed January 28, 2026, https://www.harveker.com/focus-focus-focus/.
26. Julianne Holt-Lundstad, "Lacking Social Connection Is Comparable to Smoking Up to 15 Cigarettes a Day," accessed January 28, 2026, https://www.julianneholtlunstad.com/15-cigarettes.
27. "Sitting Near a High-Performer Can Make You Better at Your Job," *KelloggInsight*, Kellogg School of Management, May 8, 2017, https://insight.kellogg.northwestern.edu/article/sitting-near-a-high-performer-can-make-you-better-at-your-job.

28. "Who Are High-Income Earners in the US and What Do They Think?" YouGov, May 17, 2024, https://yougov.com/en-us/articles/49463-who-are-high-earning-americans-and-what-do-they-think.
29. Susan Kelley, "Woulda, Coulda, Shoulda: The Haunting Regret of Failing Our Ideal Selves," *Cornell Chronicle,* Cornell University, May 24, 2018, https://news.cornell.edu/stories/2018/05/woulda-coulda-shoulda-haunting-regret-failing-our-ideal-selves.
30. Luciano Bernardi, Cesare Porta, and Peter Sleight, "Cardiovascular, Cerebrovascular, and Respiratory Changes Induced by Different Types of Music in Musicians and Non-Musicians: The Importance of Silence," *Heart* 92, no. 4 (2005): 445–452, doi:10.1136/hrt.2005.064600.
31. Sarah Garone, "8 Physical and Mental Health Benefits of Silence, Plus How to Get More of It," Healthline, September 24, 2021, https://www.healthline.com/health/mind-body/physical-and-mental-health-benefits-of-silence.
32. Imke Kirste et al., "Is Silence Golden? Effects of Auditory Stimuli and Their Absence on Adult Hippocampal Neurogenesis," *Brain Structure and Function* 220 (2015): 1221–1228, doi:10.1007/s00429-013-0679-3.
33. Garone, "8 Physical and Mental Health Benefits of Silence."
34. Joshua Becker, "21 Surprising Statistics That Reveal How Much Stuff We Actually Own," Becoming Minimalist (blog), accessed January 22, 2026, https://www.becomingminimalist.com/clutter-stats/.
35. MacVean, "Gathering Possessions Is Just the Stuff of Life."
36. Margot Adler, "Behind the Ever-Expanding American Dream House," NPR, July 4, 2006, https://www.npr.org/2006/07/04/5525283/behind-the-ever-expanding-american-dream-house.
37. Jon Mooallem, "The Self-Storage Self," *New York Times Magazine,* September 2, 2009, https://www.nytimes.com/2009/09/06/magazine/06self-storage-t.html.

38. "What Is Minimalism?," The Minimalists (blog), accessed January 28, 2026, https://www.theminimalists.com/minimalism/.
39. Joshua Fields Milburn, "Everything I Own: My 288 Things," The Minimalists (blog), https://www.theminimalists.com/288/#:~:text=That's%20everything%20I%20own.,What%20an%20amazing%20feeling
40. "Super Soul Sunday S3E2 'Oprah & Caroline Myss: Intuition, Power and Grace' | Full Episode | OWN," June 24, 2012, posted March 10, 2021, by OWN, YouTube, accessed January 22, 2026, https://www.youtube.com/watch?v=8q6txrSPWyA.

# ABOUT THE AUTHOR

Tony Caliendo is an executive coach, speaker, entrepreneur, and trusted advisor who helps high-achieving leaders, founders, and professionals answer a question that quietly haunts many of them: What if everything I have been taught about success is costing me more than it is giving?

For more than 15 years, he has watched something remarkable: The people who create the most meaningful, lasting change are not doing more—they are doing less, and with far greater clarity and courage. In a culture addicted to hustle, Tony teaches people how to identify what is draining their energy, eliminate it, and channel their focus into work and lives that feel aligned, energized, and genuinely sustainable.

He is a founding partner of reTHINK Coaching and host of the *Less Over More* podcast, where he explores the surprising power of subtraction, removing what does not belong so what matters most can finally breathe. His clients range from executives to fast-growing startup founders to ambitious professionals who are ready to stop running on empty.

Tony believes success should never feel heavy, hollow, or borrowed. It should feel like you, clear-eyed, intentional, and alive.

He lives in the Southwest with his husband, Reagan, where the wide-open spaces continue to teach him that the most important things are often the ones we almost miss.